FRESH
&GREEN

ST JOHN'S

'For years I went to Aldo's restaurant in Soho and enjoyed the spectacular food served there. He was always very generous in making sure that the vegetarian food they prepared was exquisite and I was certainly happy to be so well looked after. So it is with great pleasure that I take this opportunity to write these words and to thank Aldo and his superb team for many years of gastronomic pleasure.'

Sir Paul McCartney

FRESH & GREEN

OVER 100 EXCITING NEW VEGETARIAN RECIPES

aldo zilli

SIMON &
SCHUSTER
ILLUSTRATED

London · New York · Sydney · Toronto · New Delhi

A CBS COMPANY

First published in Great Britain in 2012 by
Simon & Schuster UK Ltd
A CBS Company
Text copyright © Aldo Zilli 2012
Design and photography © Simon & Schuster
UK Ltd 2012

Simon & Schuster Illustrated Books,
Simon & Schuster UK Ltd, 1st Floor,
222 Gray's Inn Road, London WC1X 8HB
www.simonandschuster.co.uk

Simon & Schuster Australia, Sydney
Simon & Schuster India, New Delhi

1 2 3 4 5 6 7 8 9 10

Editorial Director: Francine Lawrence
Senior Commissioning Editor: Nicky Hill
Project Editor: Sharon Brown
Designer: Isobel Gillan
Photographer: Lis Parsons
Stylist: Liz Hippisley
Food stylists: Lizzie Harris and Enzo Di Marino
Production Manager: Katherine Thornton
Commercial Director: Ami Richards

Colour reproduction by Dot Gradations Ltd, UK
Printed and bound in China

A CIP catalogue for this book is available from
the British Library.

ISBN: 978-0-85720-222-2

NOTES ON THE RECIPES

Both metric and imperial measurements have
been given in all recipes. Use one set of
measurements only and not a mixture of both.
Spoon measures are level and
1 tablespoon = 15 ml, 1 teaspoon = 5 ml.

Preheat ovens before use and cook on the
centre shelf unless cooking more than one item.

Free-range medium eggs have been used.

Both vegetarians and vegans should always
check the packaging of foods to ensure they
are suitable for them. Some cheeses are not
suitable, although alternatives can usually be
found and some vegetable stocks may not be
suitable for vegans.

This book contains recipes made with nuts.
Those with known allergic reactions to nuts and
nut derivatives, pregnant and breast-feeding
women and very young children should avoid
these dishes.

AUTHOR'S ACKNOWLEDGEMENTS

A big thank you to Francine my publisher
for believing in vegetarianism, also to Luisa
and Enzo my vegan chef for helping with the
creation, writing and testing of the recipes.
One more thanks to you the reader for taking
the time to recreate my recipes.

Contents

introduction

Gone are the days when everyone thought vegetarians only ate boring platefuls of grim-looking lentils, thank goodness. If you asked me 10 years ago to write a vegetarian cookbook I would have probably said no. But in the last five years, I have noticed a lot more people eating vegetarian and vegan food in my restaurants, even if they are not vegetarian! That list includes my wife, Nikki, and I. At home, our cooking has changed from meat or fish at every meal to mostly very tasty vegetarian dishes, such as pasta, pizza, lots of pulses and, of course, curries. I still like to cook fish and meat in my restaurants and on TV, but generally my diet is as meat-free as possible. Vegetarian cooking has become creative and inspiring with light, packed-with-flavour ideas taking inspiration from all over the world. People choose a vegetarian diet for different reasons: for some it's a health option, for others it's worries about the environment or compassion for animals.

It's far easier to follow a food lover's vegetarian diet these days as there is a vast range of soya-based products, grains, pulses and nuts to use in your cooking. Additionally, our supermarkets and markets are full of exciting fruit and vegetables from around the world, as well as our seasonal home-grown favourites, all packed with vitamins, minerals, healthy fats, fibre and antioxidants.

Growing up in Italy meant I was always surrounded by an abundance of wonderfully fresh and seasonal fruit and veg in the markets, and this has inspired many of the recipes in this book. Plus on my travels around the world I've enjoyed so many vegetarian dishes which have given me ideas for new dishes. As my mamma used to say, 'mangia le verdure' or eat your vegetables – a phrase that now takes on a whole new meaning . . .

stay healthy

Vegetarians do not eat meat, poultry or fish plus animal products such as rennet in cheese and gelatine. To keep healthy, a vegetarian diet needs to include a range of grains, pulses, nuts, fruits, vegetables, dairy and soya products. It is easy to meet your daily protein needs by eating plant-based foods, such as beans, lentils, nuts, rice and soya products like tofu and tempeh. Although there is protein in cheese, it's best not to rely on a large portion of cheese to meet your protein requirements as cheese contains saturated fat. Whole fruits and vegetables are the main source of fibre, vitamins, minerals and antioxidants, and the best way to ensure flavour and freshness is to buy seasonal produce. Calcium is also important in your overall

health, to maintain healthy teeth and bones, so include calcium-rich dairy products such as milk, cheese and yogurt in your diet.

Vegetarians also need adequate amounts of iron, zinc and vitamin B12. Iron carries oxygen in the blood and good sources include spinach, kidney beans, lentils, peas, dried apricots, prunes and raisins. Zinc helps to maintain the immune system and can be found in white beans, kidney beans, chickpeas, wheatgerm, milk and pumpkin seeds. Vitamin B12 is found in animal products but vegetarians can get it from milk products, eggs, and soya beverages. Lastly, high fibre foods are important so include bran, oatmeal, whole wheat products and couscous.

a vegan diet

As well as no meat, poultry and fish, vegans do not eat animal-derived foods such as dairy products and eggs, no animal fat of any kind, nor will they eat honey as it comes from bees. In order to stay healthy, vegans can generally stick to the same rules as vegetarians, the only main issue is vitamin B12, which can be deficient in the vegan diet. This can be solved by including vitamin B12-enriched cereal, and soya milk in the diet. For calcium, non-dairy options are soya products such as tofu, soya milk, soybeans, soya nuts, plus calcium-enriched fruit juices, and dark leafy vegetables like bok choi, broccoli, Chinese cabbage, kale and okra.

I've included some vegan recipes in this book and they are labelled. It is important as a vegan that you get into the habit of reading the food packaging labels which tell you about the product. For instance, not all vegetable stocks are suitable for vegans, so check them out before you buy.

vegetarian babies & teenagers

Breast milk or infant formula has the vitamins and minerals a baby needs; if you are vegan, there are soya-based formulas available. When weaning, start with baby rice mixed with either breast milk or formula, and then move on to puréed and sieved fruits (bananas, apples and pears are best to start with) and vegetables (such as potatoes and carrots). Don't worry if your child doesn't take to the food straight away, just keep perservering. It is best to introduce one new food at a time and wait a couple of days before trying another new food to ensure your child is not allergic to it. Make sure that you avoid gluten-based products at this stage.

Teenagers need a diet with lots of calories. Girls need 2100 calories and boys 2800 calories per day. Teenage girls should also make sure to eat iron-rich foods, try to get them to eat iron-rich and vitamin C-rich foods together. More importantly, vegan teenagers should be eating cereals and yeast extracts that contain vitamin B12. If you are not vegetarian and your child is, it is important that you still eat as a family, so make meals based on rice, potatoes and pasta which you can all enjoy.

make the most of vitamins

To ensure you get the maximum amount of vitamins, buy fruit and vegetables seasonally when they are at their best and eat them as soon as possible. Older fruit and vegetables have a lower vitamin content.

- Store your veg in a cool, dark place, as light can destroy some vitamins.
- Steam or boil your vegetables in the least amount of water possible to retain the vitamins.
- To avoid vitamin loss, don't pre-prepare your vegetables and leave them out for hours.
- Leave skin on fruit and vegetables.
- Eat food as soon as it is cooked.

what you need to include

Below is a short general guide to nutrient-rich foods. It is impossible to list all the foods so I have listed the main ones that I use.

Protein available in:
- **Nuts**: hazelnuts, brazils, walnuts, etc
- **Seeds**: sesame, pumpkin, sunflower
- **Grains**: wheat in pasta, bread and flour; barley, oats, rice
- **Soya products**: tempeh, tofu, milk
- **Dairy**: milk, cheese, yogurt
- **Eggs**
- **Pulses**: chickpeas, lentils, beans etc.

Carbohydrates available in:
- Fruit
- Milk
- Sugar

- Cereals and grains
- Root vegetables

Vitamins are in:
- **Vitamin A**: red/orange/yellow vegetables, leafy vegetables like spinach, fruits
- **Vitamin B**: wheat germ, nuts, seeds, pulses, green vegetables
- **Vitamin B12**: eggs, soya milk
- **Vitamin C**: fruits, salad leaves
- **Vitamin E**: avocado, nuts, eggs
- **Vitamin K**: cereals and vegetables

Just a word on my beloved Parmesan cheese. Some strict vegetarians do not eat all cheeses as some are made using rennet, and Parmesan is one of these. Being Italian, I love Parmesan and couldn't live without it, so I was happy to find that there are a couple of vegetarian hard cheeses on sale now which you can use instead of Parmesan as they contain no rennet. When I mention Parmesan in the recipes, I am referring to vegetarian 'Parmesan style' cheese.

I've loved writing this book, creating new ideas, and trying new seasonal flavour combinations with these delicious contemporary recipes – I hope you enjoy them too. Buon appetito!

spring

Greet the spring by enjoying
the new season's fresh veg and herbs to
add zip and flavour to your cooking.

watercress soup

with potato, onion and toasted pumpkin seeds

SERVES 4
Suitable for vegans

2 tablespoons olive oil
1 onion, chopped
1 garlic clove, crushed
1 kg (2 lb) potatoes, peeled
    and chopped
1 litre (1¾ pints) hot
    vegetable stock
150 g (5 oz) watercress
salt and freshly ground
    black pepper
4 tablespoons pumpkin
    seeds, toasted
extra virgin olive oil,
    to drizzle

The pepperiness of the watercress really lifts this soup from the ordinary, and with the added bonus that it is a natural super-food, you cannot go wrong!

1 Heat the oil in a large pan, add the onion, garlic and potatoes, and fry for 5 minutes. Pour in the stock and cook for a further 20 minutes until the potatoes are tender. Add the watercress and remove from the heat.

2 Pour the soup mixture into a blender or food processor and blitz until smooth, then season. Reheat the soup and serve in warmed bowls, topped with toasted pumpkin seeds for a crunchy texture, and a drizzle of oil.

goat's cheese gratin
with warm asparagus

SERVES 4

24–28 asparagus spears
200 g (7 oz) goat's cheese,
    sliced into four
50 g (2 oz) butter or
    margarine
freshly ground black pepper
2 tablespoons olive oil
4 tablespoons balsamic
    vinegar
75g (3 oz) baby herb leaf
    salad

Asparagus and goat's cheese make a great combination in this simple dish. I am a big fan of asparagus, which is full of vitamin K, essential for healthy bones.

1 Prepare the asparagus by peeling the stalks, if necessary, and trimming off the hard lower woody parts, about 2.5 cm (1 inch). Bring a large shallow pan of water to a simmer. Add the asparagus and cook for 4 minutes until bright green and just tender. Drain and set aside to cool slightly.

2 Place the asparagus in 4 bundles on a foil-lined baking tray. Lay a slice of goat's cheese on top of each bundle. Place a knob of the butter on top of the goat's cheese and season. Cook under a hot grill for 3 minutes until the goat's cheese is golden brown.

3 Mix together the olive oil and balsamic vinegar, and use half to dress the salad leaves. Arrange the salad in the centre of 4 serving plates, then top each with a bundle of asparagus. Drizzle the remaining dressing around the salad and serve.

beetroot soup
with lemon thyme and crème fraîche

SERVES 4

Suitable for vegans

**50 ml (2 fl oz) extra virgin
olive oil**

1 onion, chopped

1 garlic clove, crushed

1 carrot, chopped

**300 g (10 oz) potatoes, peeled
and chopped**

**1 kg (2 lb) fresh uncooked
beetroots, peeled and
chopped**

**1 tablespoon fresh lemon
thyme leaves**

**1 litre (1¾ pints) hot
vegetable stock**

**salt and freshly ground
black pepper**

**4 tablespoons crème fraîche
(optional)**

Beetroot is full of essential vitamins, and three baby beetroot equals one of the recommended 5-a-day fruit and vegetable portions for a healthy diet.

1 Heat the oil in a large pan, add the onion, garlic and carrot and fry for 5 minutes. Add the potato, beetroot and lemon thyme, pour in the stock and cook for 30 minutes until the vegetables are tender.

2 Pour the soup into a blender or food processor and blitz until smooth. Add seasoning, reheat if necessary and serve the soup in warmed bowls topped with a dollop of crème fraîche, if using.

stuffed courgette flowers
with ricotta and spinach

SERVES 4

FOR THE BATTER
80 g (3¼ oz) self-raising flour
60 g (2½ oz) cornflour
1 teaspoon salt
1 egg white
250 ml (8 fl oz) sparkling water
2 tablespoons chopped fresh parsley

FOR THE VEGETABLES
150 g (5oz) baby spinach, washed
100 g (3½ oz) ricotta cheese
15 g (½ oz) butter, diced
1 egg yolk
1 teaspoon freshly grated nutmeg
2 tablespoons freshly grated Parmesan cheese
salt and freshly ground black pepper
12 small courgettes with flowers attached
vegetable oil, for deep frying
seasoned flour, for dusting

TO SERVE
extra virgin olive oil, infused with garlic, chilli and basil

When buying courgettes, always choose small, firm ones which have a much better flavour. This recipe seems complicated but it is really easy to make.

1 To make the batter, sift the flour, cornflour and salt into a bowl. Whisk in the egg white and then the sparkling water to make a smooth batter. Add the chopped parsley and leave the batter in the fridge to rest.

2 Meanwhile, cook the spinach in a pan with the water that clings to the leaves for 3–4 minutes. Cool, squeeze out the excess water and chop the spinach. In a bowl mix the ricotta, butter, spinach, egg yolk, nutmeg and Parmesan, and season to taste.

3 Prepare the courgette flowers by pulling back the petals and removing the pollen stems. Place small spoonfuls of the spinach mixture inside the flowers, pressing it in firmly. When full, twist the top of the flower to secure the stuffing. Chill the courgettes in the fridge.

4 Heat the oil in a deep, heavy-based pan to 170°C (340°F). Dip the courgettes and stuffed flowers first in the seasoned flour and then in the batter. Drop directly into the hot oil and cook for 3–4 minutes until crispy and golden brown. Remove the fried courgettes with a slotted spoon, drain on kitchen paper and serve immediately with a dip of extra virgin olive oil infused with garlic, chilli and basil.

spinach soufflés
with melting mozzarella

SERVES 4

1 tablespoon olive oil
1 garlic clove, chopped
½ fresh chilli, deseeded
    and chopped
300 g (10 oz) cooked spinach
    (use frozen if you like)
50 ml (2 fl oz) milk
3 egg whites
50 g (2 oz) Parmesan
    cheese, grated
1 egg yolk
50 g (2 oz) butter, melted
1½ tablespoons baking
    powder
salt and freshly ground
    pepper
300 g (10 oz) plain flour
1 mozzarella cheese ball,
    cut into quarters

Rich in vitamins and minerals, spinach is essential in the vegetarian diet so we should all take a leaf out of Popeye's book and eat it regularly.

1 Preheat the oven to 180°C/fan oven 160°C/Gas Mark 4. Butter and flour 4 ramekin dishes.

2 Heat the oil in a pan, add the garlic, chilli and spinach and cook for 6 minutes. Blitz in a food processor and then add the milk and blitz again.

3 In a bowl, whisk the egg whites to form soft peaks, and then fold into the spinach mixture. Carefully fold in the Parmesan, egg yolk, butter, baking powder and seasoning. Sift the flour into the mixture and fold it in.

4 Spoon the mixture into the ramekins. Push a piece of mozzarella into the middle of each ramekin. Cook the soufflés in the oven for 11 minutes and serve immediately.

beetroot tian

with fresh orange and toasted walnuts

SERVES 4
Suitable for vegans

4 oranges
1 kg (2 lb) fresh uncooked beetroots
1 tablespoon bicarbonate of soda

TO SERVE
toasted walnuts or goat's cheese and mint

Oranges are a good source of vitamin C so together with the beetroot this is an extremely healthy dish and tastes great.

1 Grate the zest from the oranges and set aside. Cut the oranges in half and place into a large pan with the beetroots. Cover with water and add the bicarbonate of soda. Cook for 40 minutes until the beetroots are tender. Remove the oranges and beetroots from the pan and then reduce the water to 250 ml (8 fl oz) and reserve. Discard the oranges.

2 When the beetroots are cool enough to handle, peel them and slice thinly. You can either make one large tian or 4 individual tians using rings to keep the shape. Line the tin or rings with cling film. Arrange the beetroot slices in the tin or rings, sprinkling each layer with some orange zest. When finished, pour over the reserved cooking reduction liquid and refrigerate for 20 minutes before serving. Serve cold with some toasted walnuts sprinkled on top or some chopped goat's cheese and mint.

grilled tofu steaks
with asian salad

SERVES 4

Suitable for vegans

FOR THE TAMARI DRESSING

150 ml (¼ pint) tamari

2 tablespoons chopped fresh ginger

300 ml (½ pint) water

100 ml (3½ fl oz) sesame oil

1 lemongrass stalk, chopped

1 red chilli, deseeded and finely chopped

1 garlic clove, crushed

1 lime leaf

1 tablespoon chopped fresh coriander

FOR THE SALAD

400 g (13 oz) firm tofu

1 carrot, cut into ribbons

1 mooli, peeled and cut into ribbons

1 head Chinese leaves, shredded

sunflower oil, for frying

4 tablespoons cashew nuts, toasted

1 tablespoon sesame seeds

This is a great dish to serve when friends or family are coming round – both simple and impressive.

1 Blend all the ingredients for the dressing in a food processor and pour into a bowl. Slice the tofu into 8 and marinate in the dressing for 1 hour.

2 In a large bowl, mix together the carrot, mooli and Chinese leaves with some of the dressing. Heat a small amount of oil in a non-stick pan, remove the tofu from the dressing and pan-fry it for 2 minutes on each side.

3 Divide the salad mixture between 4 serving plates and arrange the pan-fried tofu on top. Sprinkle over the cashew nuts and sesame seeds, drizzle over any remaining dressing and serve.

Zilli know-how

Tamari is a rich, dark, wheat-free version of soy sauce so it is suitable for those with wheat allergies. You can use dark soy sauce in this recipe if you prefer.

mexican chilli beans
with stir-fried tempeh

SERVES 4
Suitable for vegans

4 tablespoons olive oil

2 sticks celery, diced

2 shallots, diced

1 carrot, diced

1 teaspoon chopped garlic

1 teaspoon ground cumin

1 teaspoon ground coriander

1 tablespoon smoked
   paprika

100 ml (3½ fl oz) water

100 ml (3½ fl oz) red wine

2 x 390 g cartons or cans
   black or kidney beans,
   rinsed and drained

150 ml (¼ pint) hot
   vegetable stock

1 tablespoon tomato purée

salt and freshly ground
   black pepper

2 tablespoons sunflower oil

100 g (3½ oz) tempeh, cut in
   pieces and marinated in
   100 ml (3½ fl oz) tamari or
   soy sauce

1 handful chopped fresh
   coriander, plus extra

1 handful chopped fresh
   oregano

2 red chillies, deseeded and
   finely chopped

juice of 1 lime

4 tablespoons crème fraîche
   (optional)

This spicy favourite is good for a casual get-together with friends. You can make the bean mixture ahead.

1 Heat the olive oil in a large pan and cook the celery, shallots, carrot and garlic for 5 minutes. Stir in the cumin, coriander and paprika and cook for a further 2 minutes, and then add the water. Add the red wine and reduce the mixture for 5 minutes.

2 Add the drained beans and stock to the vegetables and cook for a further 10 minutes. Add the tomato purée and seasoning and cook for 10 minutes.

3 In a separate pan, heat the sunflower oil and stir-fry the tempeh for 4 minutes and then add to the bean mixture with the coriander, oregano, chillies and lime juice. Cook the chilli for 2 minutes and serve with a dollop of crème fraîche, if using, and steamed rice, garnished with coriander sprigs.

Zilli know-how

Tempeh is a cultured product made from soya beans and is a good source of protein for vegetarians and vegans. It has a savoury, nutty flavour and firm texture, and is available chilled or frozen from health food shops. Tempeh can be used in stir-fries, casseroles, salads and bakes. If you can't find tempeh, serve the spicy beans with quinoa.

spaghetti with juniper berries

SERVES 4

1 litre (1¾ pints) red wine
10 juniper berries
1 bay leaf
1 fresh rosemary sprig
4 tablespoons caster sugar
2 tablespoons butter
1 head radicchio, thinly
   sliced
salt and freshly ground
   black pepper
100 ml (3½ fl oz) cream
500 g (1 lb) spaghetti
1 tablespoon chopped
   fresh parsley

Juniper berries have a deliciously different flavour that makes this dish really special. You can add some blue cheese if you want an extra kick.

1 Pour the wine into a large pan, add the juniper berries, bay leaf, rosemary and sugar, and boil to reduce to approximately 100 ml (3½ fl oz) then strain.

2 In another pan, melt the butter, add the radicchio and cook for 5 minutes. Season, stir in the cream and cook the sauce for 4 more minutes.

3 Meanwhile, cook the spaghetti according to packet instructions. Drain the pasta and mix with the radicchio sauce. Cook for 1 minute, then add the parsley and 2 tablespoons of the strained wine reduction. (The remaining reduction can be kept in the fridge and used for another dish.) Divide the spaghetti between 4 warmed plates and serve.

nettle and shallot risotto

SERVES 4

200 g (7 oz) fresh nettle tops,
  well washed
2 tablespoons extra virgin
  olive oil
50 g (2 oz) butter
2 banana shallots, finely
  chopped
1 garlic clove, crushed
325 g (11 oz) arborio
  risotto rice
250 ml (8 fl oz) white wine
1.5 litres (2½ pints) hot
  vegetable stock or cooking
  water from the nettles
salt and freshly ground
  black pepper
3 tablespoons chopped
  fresh parsley
2 tablespoons freshly grated
  Parmesan cheese

This unusual risotto has a great taste which is like a combination of spinach, sorrel and green bean flavours. Amazingly healthy nettles are also good in soups.

1 Using tongs pick up the nettles, place them in boiling salted water and blanch for 40 seconds. Strain the nettles, reserving the water if using later, then place nettles in a blender or food processor and blitz to form a paste, adding some of the cooking water if the mixture is too thick.

2 Heat the oil and half the butter in a large, deep frying pan, add the shallots and fry gently for 5 minutes until soft. Add the garlic and cook for a further 2 minutes. Add the rice and stir until the rice is glistening with butter. Add the wine and cook until all the wine has been absorbed.

3 In a separate pan, bring the stock to a simmer.

4 Add a ladleful of hot stock to the rice and cook over a moderate heat for 3–5 minutes, stirring, until the liquid is absorbed. Add the nettle paste, stir well and season.

5 Continue adding the stock, a ladleful at a time, until all or nearly all the stock has been used and the rice is tender (this should take about 18 minutes in total).

6 When the risotto is ready, remove from the heat and stir in the remaining butter, parsley and grated cheese. The finished risotto should be quite fluffy but not soupy. Cover and leave to stand for 1 minute before serving.

tuscan pulse and grain stew

SERVES 4
Suitable for vegans

2 tablespoons extra virgin
   olive oil, plus extra
3 smoked garlic cloves,
   finely chopped
1 onion, finely diced
1 stick celery, finely diced
1 carrot, finely diced
1 tablespoon finely chopped
   rosemary
1 tablespoon finely chopped
   sage
1 tablespoon finely chopped
   thyme
100 g (3½ oz) spelt grain
100 g (3½ oz) dried
   chickpeas, soaked
   overnight and drained
2 litres (3½ pints) hot
   vegetable stock, plus extra
100 g (3½ oz) barley
100 g (3½ oz) lentils
1 fennel bulb, diced
3 plum tomatoes, deseeded
   and chopped
salt and freshly ground
   black pepper
grated zest and juice of
   1 lemon
1 tablespoon finely chopped
   fresh parsley
2 tablespoons freshly
   grated Parmesan cheese
   (optional)

Spelt is available in health food stores and is becoming more popular in vegetarian cooking due to its high protein content. This is a delicious simple stew.

1 Heat the oil in a large pan or casserole and fry the garlic, onion, celery, carrot, rosemary, sage and thyme for 2 minutes over a low heat.

2 Stir in the spelt, drained chickpeas and the stock and cook for 15 minutes. Add the barley, lentils, fennel and tomatoes and cook for a further 1 hour until the barley and chickpeas are cooked, adding extra stock if necessary. Season to taste.

3 Remove from the heat and add the lemon zest and juice. Sprinkle over the parsley and cheese, if using, and drizzle over a little extra virgin olive oil. Serve with crusty bread.

the zilli salad

SERVES 4

FOR THE DRESSING

**75 ml (3 fl oz) extra virgin
   olive oil**
**25 ml (1 fl oz) white wine
   vinegar**
1 garlic clove, crushed
1 teaspoon Dijon mustard
**salt and freshly ground
   black pepper**

FOR THE SALAD

**150 g (5 oz) feta cheese,
   cut into large dice**
**60 g (2½ oz) stoned kalamata
   olives**
**60 g (2½ oz) sundried
   tomatoes, cut into strips**
**100 g (3½ oz) cucumber,
   cut into strips**
**100 g (3½ oz) carrots,
   cut into strips**
**150 g (5 oz) baby salad
   leaves**

This is my favourite salad. The secret is the dressing which pulls all the wonderful flavours together.

1 Pour all the ingredients for the dressing into a bowl and whisk well together.

2 Place all the salad ingredients in a large bowl, pour over the dressing and toss everything together until well mixed. Serve the salad immediately.

pancake lasagne

SERVES 6

FOR THE PANCAKES
2 medium eggs
300 ml (½ pint) milk
2 tablespoons sunflower oil
125 g (4 oz) plain flour

FOR THE VEGGIE BALLS
50 ml (2 fl oz) sunflower oil
1 onion, finely chopped
1 stick celery, finely chopped
100 g (3½ oz) carrots, finely chopped
1 tablespoon mixed dried herbs
1 tablespoon chopped fresh rosemary
1 tablespoon chopped fresh thyme
200 g (7 oz) soya mince, rehydrated following packet instructions
250 ml (8 fl oz) red wine
1 litre (1¾ pints) water
2 teaspoons fennel seeds
2 teaspoons tomato purée
200 g (7 oz) couscous
1 tablespoon chopped fresh parsley
salt and freshly ground pepper

This is a version of the lasagne my sister-in-law in Italy makes when I visit. It's very tasty and pancakes make it much lighter than the usual pasta version.

1 To make the pancakes, mix the eggs, milk and half of the oil in a jug. Sift the flour into a bowl and gradually beat in the egg mixture to make a smooth batter. Heat an 18 cm (7 inch) frying pan and brush some of the remaining oil over the base. Pour an eighth of the batter into the pan, swirling it around to spread it over the base. Cook for 1–2 minutes until the batter is set and golden on the base. Flip over and cook for a further 1–2 minutes until golden on the other side. Repeat with the remaining mixture to make 8 pancakes. Set aside.

2 To make the veggie balls, heat the oil in a large pan and cook the onion, celery, carrots, dried herbs, rosemary and thyme until the onion is golden. Add the rehydrated soya mince and wine and cook for 2 minutes. Add the water, fennel seeds and tomato purée and cook for 20 minutes. When the soya has softened, remove from the heat and stir in the couscous. Cover and set aside for 15 minutes until the couscous is cooked. Add the parsley, season and shape the mixture into 1 cm (½ inch) balls.

3 To make the tomato sauce, heat the oil in a frying pan, add the onion and garlic and cook for 3 minutes until soft but not browned. Add the passata and simmer for 10 minutes, then add the veggie balls and cook for a further 10 minutes.

4 To make the béchamel, melt the butter in a small pan, add the flour and cook for 1 minute, stirring continuously. Add the milk a little at a time, stirring (or whisking) to ensure there are no lumps. Continue adding the milk to make a smooth sauce.

SPRING lunch dishes

FOR THE TOMATO SAUCE

1 tablespoon extra virgin olive oil

1 onion, finely chopped

1 garlic clove, finely chopped

500 g jar passata

FOR THE BECHAMEL SAUCE

25 g (1 oz) unsalted butter

25 g (1 oz) plain flour

150 ml (¼ pint) milk

salt and freshly ground black pepper

beaten egg and freshly grated Parmesan cheese, to finish

5 Preheat the oven to 180°C/fan oven 160°C/Gas Mark 4. Spread some of the béchamel over the bottom of a medium-size baking dish or tin. Cover with a layer of pancakes and then a layer of veggie balls and tomato sauce. Add some more béchamel, drizzle with beaten egg and sprinkle with some cheese. Continue layering in this way, finishing with a layer of pancakes. Spread any remaining béchamel, egg and tomato sauce over the top, sprinkle with grated cheese and bake for 30 minutes until bubbling and golden.

spelt pizza
with asparagus and blue cheese

SERVES 4

FOR THE BASE
335 ml (11½ fl oz) warm
    water
7 g (¼ oz) dried yeast
pinch of sugar
540 g (1 lb 2 oz) white spelt
    flour
7 g (¼ oz) salt
60 ml (2½ fl oz) extra virgin
    olive oil
2 pinches of dried oregano

FOR THE TOPPING
400 g can chopped tomatoes
½ teaspoon dried oregano
½ teaspoon dried basil
1 teaspoon salt
2 tablespoons extra virgin
    olive oil, plus extra to
    drizzle
6 asparagus spears,
    cut in half
2 mozzarella cheese balls,
    sliced
100 g (3½ oz) blue cheese,
    crumbled
50 g (2 oz) freshly grated
    Parmesan cheese
fresh oregano sprigs

White spelt flour is ideal for pastry and bread-making, and here it adds a lovely nutty flavour to this pizza. If you can't find spelt flour you can use '00' flour instead.

1 To make the base, mix the water with the yeast and sugar and leave in a warm place for 15 minutes. Sift the flour and salt into a large bowl, add the yeast mixture, oil and oregano and mix well to make a dough.

2 Divide the dough into 4 equal portions and form each into a 10 cm (4 inch) diameter ball. Leave to rest for 20 minutes.

3 To make the topping, combine the chopped tomatoes with the dried oregano, basil, salt and olive oil and mix well. Lightly blanch the asparagus in boiling water for 3 minutes.

4 Preheat the oven to 240°C/fan oven 220°C/Gas Mark 9, or as hot as possible. Knead and roll out the dough to make 4 thin bases. Spread over the tomato sauce and top with the mozzarella slices. Arrange the asparagus and crumbled blue cheese on top. Drizzle with extra olive oil and sprinkle over the Parmesan. Cook for 8–10 minutes, top with the oregano sprigs and serve straight away.

spring vegetable frittata

SERVES 3–4

2 tablespoons extra virgin
   olive oil
1 onion, finely sliced
400 g (13 oz) spring
   vegetables such as
   peppers, purple sprouting
   broccoli, watercress and
   asparagus, diced
175 g (6 oz) fresh shelled
   broad beans, blanched and
   skins removed
6 eggs
2 tablespoons chopped fresh
   parsley
50 g (2 oz) pecorino cheese,
   grated
salt and freshly ground
   black pepper

Growing up in Italy we had this a lot as it is relatively inexpensive and tasty and can feed a lot of people. You can also use up leftover roast vegetables from the fridge.

1 Heat the oil in a large frying pan and cook the onion for about 8 minutes over a low heat. Add the spring vegetables and cook for a further 2 minutes, then add the broad beans.

2 In a bowl, beat together the eggs, parsley and pecorino with some seasoning. Pour into the frying pan and cook over a low heat for about 10 minutes, shaking the pan often to make sure the frittata doesn't stick. Place under a hot grill for 2 minutes to finish the cooking. Cool slightly before serving cut into slices.

warm jerusalem artichoke tart
with rosemary and dolcelatte

SERVES 8

FOR THE PASTRY
250 g (8 oz) plain flour
pinch of salt
125 g (4 oz) butter, cut into pieces
a little very finely chopped rosemary
1 egg yolk
100 ml (3½ fl oz) cold water

FOR THE FILLING
400 g (13 oz) Jerusalem artichokes
4 tablespoons olive oil
100 g (3½ oz) shallots, chopped
1 tablespoon chopped fresh rosemary
150 ml (¼ pint) double cream
2 eggs
2 egg yolks
salt and freshly ground pepper
150 g (5 oz) dolcelatte cheese, cut into pieces

This tart can be made in advance. I like to eat this with a nice leafy salad with a mustard dressing. You can use ready-made shortcrust pastry if time's short.

1 To make the pastry, tip the flour and salt into a bowl. Add the butter and rub it in with your fingertips until the mixture is crumbly. Stir in the rosemary then mix in the egg yolk and water to form a dough.

2 Preheat the oven to 180°C/fan oven 160°C/Gas Mark 4. Roll out the pastry on a lightly floured surface and then use it to line a 23 cm (9 inch) tart tin. Line the pastry case with baking paper or foil and fill with baking beans. Cook the pastry case for 10 minutes. Remove the paper or foil and beans and cook for a further 5–10 minutes until golden.

3 To make the filling, peel and finely slice the artichokes. Heat the oil in a pan and fry the shallots, rosemary and artichokes for 5–10 minutes until soft.

4 In a bowl, beat together the cream, eggs, yolks and seasoning. Stir in the artichoke mixture. Pour the filling into the pastry case and sprinkle over the chopped dolcelatte. Cook the tart for 15 minutes until golden. Leave to cool a little then cut into slices and serve warm with a crisp salad.

mushroom wellington
with baby vegetables

SERVES 4

FOR THE VEGETABLES

1 bunch baby carrots

1 bunch baby fennel

1 bunch baby beetroot

1 bunch baby leeks

olive oil, to drizzle

**salt and freshly ground
    black pepper**

**1 kg (2 lb) red onions, cut
    in quarters**

**50 ml (2 fl oz) balsamic
    vinegar**

100 g (3½ oz) caster sugar

FOR THE MUSHROOM
    WELLINGTON

4 tablespoons olive oil

**500 g (1 lb) button
    mushrooms, quartered**

1 garlic clove, crushed

1 shallot, chopped

**½ head spring greens, thinly
    sliced and steamed**

**150 g (5 oz) fresh
    breadcrumbs**

200 g (7 oz) ground almonds

**4 tablespoons chopped fresh
    parsley**

**500 g pack ready-rolled puff
    pastry sheet**

If you can get some wild mushrooms in season, add them to this recipe for a richer flavour. A special choice for entertaining.

1 Wash and steam all the baby vegetables until just tender and drizzle with a little olive oil. Season and keep warm.

2 Preheat the oven to 180°C/fan oven 160°C/Gas Mark 4. Place the red onions on a baking tray and drizzle with a little oil. Cover with foil and cook for 30 minutes. Remove the foil and sprinkle over the balsamic vinegar and caster sugar and cook for a further 15 minutes. Keep warm.

3 To make the mushroom wellington, heat the oil in a large pan and fry the mushrooms for about 10 minutes until all the water from the mushrooms has evaporated. Add the garlic and shallot and cook for a further 5 minutes. Remove from the heat and add the spring greens, breadcrumbs and almonds. Cook for 5 minutes and then add the parsley and season.

4 Increase the oven temperature to 200°C/fan oven 180°C/Gas Mark 6. Lay the pastry sheet on a lined baking tray. Spoon the mushroom filling down the centre lengthways and then make 3 cm (1¼ inch) cuts down both sides of the pastry and plait the pastry strips alternately over the filling. Cook in the oven for 25 minutes. Serve cut into slices, with the baby vegetables and caramelised red onions. This dish is good served with Mushroom gravy (see page165).

seaweed caviar bruschetta and sushi rolls

SERVES 4
Suitable for vegans

400 g (13 oz) sushi rice
1 tablespoon rice vinegar
1 tablespoon mirin
1 tablespoon sake
salt
4 nori sheets
1 avocado, thinly sliced
1 tablespoon butter
**1 small baguette, sliced into
  very thin slices**
**4 tablespoons seaweed
  caviar**
**wasabi and pickled ginger,
  to serve**

I love Japanese food. Seaweed caviar is a great addition to this veggie sushi as it gives that salty, sea flavour.

1 Cook the rice according to packet instructions, then remove from the heat and cover for 10 minutes. Stir in the rice vinegar, mirin, sake and salt to taste.

2 Place a nori sheet on a sushi rolling mat or sheet of heavy foil. With damp hands, place one quarter of the rice on the nori and press down so that it covers the nori. Add one quarter of the avocado slices on top of the rice and roll up. Repeat with the remaining rice, avocado and nori sheets.

3 Spread the butter on the bread, and then toast under a hot grill. Add a little seaweed caviar to each slice.

4 Slice each sushi roll into 8 rounds and serve with wasabi, pickled ginger and the caviar bruschetta.

Zilli know-how

Seaweed caviar is a product from Sweden which looks and tastes like caviar but is made from seaweed. Red and black varieties are available and both are good for this recipe. Make sure the brand you buy is suitable for vegetarians.

plantain skewers

SERVES 5
Suitable for vegans

4 plantain
1 red chilli, deseeded and
    finely chopped
1 bunch coriander, finely
    chopped
zest and juice of 1 lemon
salt and freshly ground
    black pepper
10 lemongrass stalks
200 g (7 oz) polenta flour

The reason you use lemongrass skewers is that as you cook them, the flavour of the lemongrass infuses the plantain to give it a lovely lemony flavour.

1 Put the unpeeled plantain in a pan, cover with cold water, bring to the boil and cook for 4 minutes. Drain the plantain and remove the skin.

2 Mash the plantain with the chilli, coriander, lemon zest and juice. Mix well and season.

3 Preheat the oven to 190°C/fan oven 170°C/Gas Mark 5. Divide the plantain mixture into 8–10 balls and mould around the lemongrass stalks. Dust with polenta flour, lay on a baking tray and cook for 15 minutes. Serve immediately.

Zilli know-how

Plantains are a Caribbean ingredient and look like long bananas and, when ripe, the skin is black. They cannot be eaten raw and are best grilled, fried, boiled or barbecued.

the zilli veggie burger

SERVES 6
Suitable for vegans

4 tablespoons olive oil
1 onion, chopped
1 stick celery, chopped
100 g (3½ oz) carrots,
   chopped
1 tablespoon mixed dried
   herbs
1 tablespoon chopped fresh
   rosemary
1 tablespoon chopped fresh
   thyme
200 g (7 oz) soya mince,
   rehydrated following
   packet instructions
250 ml (8 fl oz) red wine
1 litre (1¾ pints) water
2 teaspoons fennel seeds
2 teaspoons tomato purée
200 g (7 oz) couscous
1 tablespoon chopped fresh
   parsley
salt and freshly ground
   black pepper

TO SERVE
6 burger buns
homemade mayo and
   ketchup (see page 44),
   mixed salad leaves, sliced
   avocado and tomatoes,
   and gherkins

These burgers are always popular with family and friends. You can add some mozzarella and chilli to make them into chilli cheese burgers!

1 Heat 2 tablespoons of the oil in a pan and cook the onion, celery, carrots, mixed dried herbs, rosemary and thyme until the onion is golden. Add the soya mince and red wine and cook for 2 minutes.

2 Add the water, fennel seeds and tomato purée to the pan and cook for 20 minutes. When the soya has softened, remove the pan from the heat and stir in the couscous. Cover and leave for 15 minutes until the couscous is cooked. Add the parsley and seasoning and shape into 6 burgers.

3 Heat the remaining oil in a frying pan and fry the burgers for 2 minutes on each side until golden brown. Serve the burgers in buns with some homemade mayonnaise and ketchup, salad leaves, sliced avocado, tomatoes and gherkins.

mayonnaise

SERVES 10
Suitable for vegans

250 ml (8 fl oz) soya milk

1 teaspoon salt

50 ml (2 fl oz) apple cider
  vinegar

juice of 1 lemon

1 tablespoon English
  mustard

pinch of sugar

500 ml (18 fl oz) sunflower
  oil

Whisk the milk with the salt, vinegar, lemon juice, mustard and sugar. Add the oil slowly, whisking all the time. Cover and chill in the refrigerator.

homemade ketchup

SERVES 10
Suitable for vegans

3 tablespoons olive oil

1 onion, chopped

1 kg (2 lb) plum tomatoes,
  chopped

225 g (7½ oz) sugar

250 ml (8 fl oz) white wine
  vinegar

salt and freshly ground
  black pepper

Heat the oil in a pan and fry the onion for a few minutes. Add the plum tomatoes and cook for 20 minutes. Stir in the sugar, vinegar and seasoning. Blitz in a blender, then pass through a sieve. Cover and chill in the refrigerator.

sweet potato and smoky tofu spring rolls

SERVES 4

200 g (7 oz) sweet potato, diced
1 tablespoon olive oil
1 tablespoon vegetable oil, plus extra for deep frying
1 shallot, finely chopped
400 g (13 oz) smoked tofu
splash of soy sauce
1 tablespoon chopped fresh coriander
4 tablespoons pine nuts
4 tablespoons cream cheese
8 spring roll wrappers
tamari soy sauce, to serve

This makes a really tasty starter and although you can serve the rolls with a sweet chilli dipping sauce, the tamari sauce makes the flavours come together.

1 Preheat the oven to 180°C/fan oven 160°C/Gas Mark 4. Place the sweet potato in a roasting tin and toss in the olive oil. Roast in the oven for 10 minutes.

2 Heat the vegetable oil in a pan and fry the chopped shallot for 3 minutes. Crush the tofu in your hands, add it to the pan and cook for 4 minutes. Add the soy sauce and cook for a further 3 minutes. Add the coriander and pine nuts. Remove from the heat and stir in the cream cheese.

3 Lay the spring roll wrappers on a work surface and place a generous tablespoonful of the tofu mixture on one side of each sheet. Fold up the end over the filling, fold in the sides and then roll up, sticking with water.

4 Heat the oil in a deep, heavy-based pan and deep-fry the spring rolls for 3–4 minutes until golden. Serve with tamari soy sauce on the side.

rhubarb tart tatin

SERVES 6

200 g (7 oz) ready-made
    puff pastry
15 g (½ oz) unsalted butter,
    softened
125 g (4 oz) granulated sugar
zest of 1 orange
1 teaspoon ground cinnamon
1 tablespoon vanilla extract
700 g (1 lb 7 oz) rhubarb,
    cut into chunks
100 g (3½ oz) mascarpone
    cheese
100 g (3½ oz) ricotta cheese

Most people assume that rhubarb is a fruit but it is a very sour vegetable. You need a lot of sugar when using rhubarb so that you end up with a tart, sweet flavour.

1 Preheat the oven to 190°C/fan oven 170°C/Gas Mark 5. Roll out the pastry and cut out a circle slightly larger than a 20 cm (8 inch) ovenproof frying pan. Prick the pastry circle all over and chill for 1 hour.

2 Spread the base of the frying pan with the butter and sprinkle over the sugar, orange zest, cinnamon and vanilla. Top with the rhubarb. Cook over a high heat for 10 minutes to caramelise and cook the rhubarb until tender – check by piercing a piece with a knife but do not stir!

3 Cover the pan with the pastry, tucking it down the inside of the pan. Cook for 20–30 minutes in the oven until the pastry is golden and cooked. Remove from the oven and leave to rest for a few minutes, then invert a plate over the top and turn out the tart. In a bowl, mix together the mascarpone and ricotta and serve with the warm tart tatin.

vegan chocolate cake

SERVES 8
Suitable for vegans

200 g (7 oz) plain flour
200 g (7 oz) caster sugar
20 g (¾ oz) cocoa powder
1 teaspoon bicarbonate
 of soda
1 teaspoon salt
75 ml (3 fl oz) melted
 Pure spread
1 teaspoon vanilla extract
1 teaspoon white vinegar
235 ml (7½ fl oz) water
ice cream, to serve

This is a very simple recipe that works every time, and proves that vegans can indulge their sweet tooth.

1 Preheat the oven to 180°C/fan oven 160°C/Gas Mark 4. Lightly grease and line a 23 x 13cm (9 x 5 inch) loaf tin.

2 In a large bowl, sift together the flour, sugar, cocoa, bicarbonate of soda and salt. Add the spread, vanilla, vinegar and water, and mix well until smooth.

3 Pour the cake mixture into the prepared tin and bake for 45 minutes until cooked. Remove from the oven and allow to cool then turn out onto a cooling rack. Serve warm with scoops of ice cream or as a teatime treat.

minted fruit
with rosemary mascarpone

SERVES 4

small sprig fresh rosemary
60 ml (2½ fl oz) single cream
250 g (8 oz) mascarpone
  cheese
1 tablespoon icing sugar
1 vanilla pod, split and seeds
  removed
1 pear, cored, peeled and
  sliced
2 mangoes, stoned, peeled
  and sliced
½ melon, deseeded and
  chopped
1 sprig fresh mint
1 teaspoon lemon juice
1 tablespoon orange juice

It's unusual to use rosemary in a dessert, but it goes brilliantly with the mascarpone. You can also serve the rosemary mascarpone with your favourite poached fruits.

1 Strip the leaves off the rosemary sprig and chop finely. In a bowl, mix together the cream, mascarpone, icing sugar, vanilla seeds and rosemary. Cover and chill in the refrigerator until needed.

2 Mix all the fruit together in a bowl. Finely chop the mint and add to the bowl. Add the lemon and orange juices and toss all the fruit together. Serve the fruit salad with dollops of rosemary mascarpone on the top.

cappuccino mousse
with banana slices

SERVES 4

**397g can sweetened
    condensed milk**
40 g (1½ oz) butter
2 teaspoons espresso coffee
**30 g (1½ oz) cocoa powder,
    plus extra for sprinkling**
2 bananas, peeled and sliced
**450 ml (16 fl oz) double
    cream**

Coffee and banana – it doesn't get better than this! I call this cappuccino as it looks like one. Serve in a coffee cup if you want to impress your friends.

1 In a saucepan, combine the condensed milk, butter and coffee and stir over a low heat for 1 minute. Stir in the cocoa and cook until the butter has melted and the mixture is smooth. Remove from the heat and stir in the banana slices. Leave to cool.

2 In a bowl, whip the cream to soft peaks and then fold into the coffee mixture. Spoon into coffee cups and refrigerate until set. Dust with cocoa powder just before serving.

summer

Now's the time for eating out of doors,
enjoying the long, warm days and
the fabulous flavours of summer.

gazpacho soup
with heritage tomatoes

SERVES 4
Suitable for vegans

1 garlic clove
½ small red onion, chopped
½ red pepper, deseeded and chopped
½ green pepper, deseeded and chopped
1 cucumber, peeled and chopped
2 slices white bread
300 ml (½ pint) tomato juice
300 g (10 oz) heritage tomatoes, chopped
1 tablespoon extra virgin olive oil
1 teaspoon white wine vinegar
½ teaspoon sea salt
¼ teaspoon ground black pepper

TO SERVE
ice cubes
basil sprigs
chopped red and green peppers
croûtons

This classic Spanish soup is popular the world over. It's perfect for a hot day as the coldness of the dish, along with the acidic bite, refreshes you in the heat of summer.

1 Place all the ingredients in a blender or food processor and blitz until smooth. Chill the soup in the fridge until you're ready to serve.

2 Serve the soup in bowls, garnished with ice cubes and basil sprigs, with chopped peppers and croûtons.

Zilli know-how

Heritage or heirloom vegetables are traditional varieties which are now being grown again – look out for them at farmers' markets. *Heritage tomatoes* come in all shapes and sizes, they may not look as perfect as their supermarket friends but the flavour is often far superior.

sorrel soup
with potato and garlic

SERVES 4
Suitable for vegans

1 head garlic
2 tablespoons olive oil
1 onion, chopped
1 kg (2 lb) potatoes, peeled
 and cubed
1 tablespoon cumin seeds
1.2 litres (2 pints) hot
 vegetable stock
200 g (7 oz) sorrel, chopped
salt and freshly ground
 black pepper
extra virgin olive oil,
 to drizzle

The tanginess of the sorrel makes this soup great as a summer dish as it lightens the soup and makes it perfect for a starter.

1 Preheat the oven to 180°C/fan oven 160°C/Gas Mark 4. Bake the head of garlic in the oven for 20 minutes and, when nice and soft, squeeze out the pulp with a fork.

2 Heat the oil in a pan and cook the onion, potatoes and cumin seeds for 5 minutes. Cover with the stock and cook for a further 20 minutes. Add the sorrel and garlic pulp and cook for 10 minutes. Season, then blitz the soup in a blender or food processor and serve in warmed bowls with a drizzle of extra virgin olive oil.

Zilli know-how

Sorrel looks a bit like spinach and the young leaves have a fruity flavour, while the older leaves are more acidic. Young leaves are good for salads and when lightly cooked. The older leaves are better for soups and stews as they add a tang.

grilled halloumi
on caesar salad

SERVES 4

150 g (5 oz) halloumi
   cheese, sliced

FOR THE DRESSING
1 egg
2 garlic cloves
2 tablespoons lemon juice
125 ml (4 fl oz) extra virgin
   olive oil, plus extra for
   brushing
1 cos lettuce, torn into
   pieces
150g (5 oz) herb croûtons
75 g (3 oz) Parmesan cheese,
   half grated and half
   shaved

Halloumi is a salty Cypriot cheese. It has a higher melting point than most cheeses, which means it holds together when grilling and so is perfect for this dish.

1 To make the Caesar dressing, blend the egg, garlic and lemon juice in a food processor. Add the olive oil in a steady stream, as if making mayonnaise – when the mixture thickens it is ready. Pour the dressing into a jug and chill in the fridge until ready to use.

2 In a large bowl, mix together the lettuce, croûtons, grated Parmesan and dressing, combining well so that the dressing is evenly distributed.

3 Heat a griddle pan until nearly smoking. Brush some oil over the halloumi slices and grill for 40 seconds on each side.

4 Divide the salad between 4 serving plates, lay the halloumi on top and sprinkle over the shaved Parmesan.

artichoke, samphire and courgette tempura

300 g (10 oz) rice flour
1 level teaspoon salt
1 egg
700 ml (1¼ pints) light beer
   or sparkling water
4 violet artichokes
100 g (3½ oz) samphire
100 g (3½ oz) courgettes
vegetable oil, for frying
100 ml (3½ fl oz) milk
100 ml (3½ fl oz) soy sauce
1 tablespoon chopped fresh
   coriander
2 limes, quartered

I prefer to use artichokes in this recipe but sweet potato, broccoli and cauliflower all work well too.

1 In a large bowl, mix together 225 g (7½ oz) of the rice flour, the salt and egg, and then add the beer or water, a little at a time, until the batter is smooth and lump-free. Leave the batter in the fridge for 20–25 minutes.

2 Trim and quarter the artichokes and remove the tough middle parts. Thoroughly rinse, drain and dry the samphire. Trim and cut the courgettes into chunky strips.

3 Heat the oil in a deep, heavy-based pan to 170°C (340°F). Dip the vegetables into the milk, coat them in the remaining rice flour and then dip the vegetables into the batter, making sure they are completely covered. Fry the vegetables in batches for 2–3 minutes until golden.

4 Mix together the soy sauce, 2 tablespoons still water and coriander, and spoon into a ramekin as a dipping sauce. Serve the tempura with the sauce and a squeeze of lime.

Zilli know-how

You can use normal flour for this recipe but **rice flour** makes the tempura crisper.

Once described as the poor man's asparagus, **samphire** is a wild coastal plant which is fast becoming a 'trendy' garnish in many top restaurants. That said, it is a fantastic vegetable in its own right and can be made into a wonderful pickled vegetable.

Violet artichokes, also called French artichokes, are easy to cook with as they have no spines and no hairy choke. They are smaller and more tender than other artichokes.

broad bean salad
with pecorino and rocket

SERVES 4

600 g (1 lb 4 oz) broad
   beans, shelled
100 g (3½ oz) wild rocket,
   washed
3 tablespoons olive oil
juice of 1 lemon
salt and freshly ground
   black pepper
100 g (3½ oz) pecorino
   cheese, shaved
2 tomatoes, finely chopped
½ red onion, finely sliced

Fresh broad beans are best for this salad but if you can't find them, use frozen beans and treat in the same way. Make sure you remove the bitter outer skin.

1 Cook the broad beans in boiling water for 5 minutes and drain. Remove the outer skin and place the beans in a large salad bowl. Roughly chop the rocket and add to the bowl.

2 In a small bowl, whisk together the oil, lemon juice and seasoning, and add to the salad with the cheese, tomatoes and onion, tossing all the ingredients together before serving.

tomato and rye bruschetta

SERVES 4
Suitable for vegans

2 medium onions, diced
1 garlic clove, finely diced
2 tablespoons chopped
   fresh basil
7 heritage tomatoes, diced
3 tablespoons olive oil, plus
   extra for drizzling
1 tablespoon balsamic
   vinegar
1 rye bread loaf

When I got home from school my mamma would make me bruschetta to keep me going until dinner. Now I make them as a snack when friends come round.

1 Mix together the onions, garlic, basil and tomatoes. Whisk the oil and vinegar, toss into the onion mixture and leave to marinate for at least 1 hour.

2 Preheat the grill to high. Slice the rye bread and brush lightly with olive oil. Grill the bread on each side and serve topped with the tomato mixture.

thai-style grilled vegetables

SERVES 4
Suitable for vegans

FOR THE DRESSING
**150 ml (¼ pint) tamari
soy sauce**
**2 tablespoons chopped
fresh ginger**
300 ml (½ pint) water
100 ml (3½ fl oz) sesame oil
1 lemongrass stalk, chopped
**1 red chilli, deseeded and
chopped**
1 garlic clove, crushed
1 lime leaf, chopped
**1 tablespoon chopped fresh
coriander**

FOR THE VEGETABLES
**1 aubergine, trimmed and
sliced lengthways**
**3 courgettes, trimmed and
sliced**
**1 red pepper, deseeded
and sliced**
1 red onion, sliced

If you are having friends round for lunch, this is the perfect dish to make and leave on the table for them to pick at or you can use it as part of an antipasto dish.

1 In a bowl, blend all the dressing ingredients together and pour into a small jug.

2 Heat a griddle pan and grill all the vegetables until just tender. Cover the sliced vegetables with the dressing and serve either warm or cold.

taleggio and pistachio stuffed peppers

SERVES 4

4 large red peppers
salt and freshly ground
    black pepper
3 tablespoons extra virgin
    olive oil
250 g (8 oz) red rice
100 g (3½ oz) Taleggio
    cheese, cubed
100 g (3½ oz) mascarpone
    cheese
100 g (3½ oz) pistachio nuts
3 tablespoons chopped
    spring onions
3 tablespoons freshly grated
    Parmesan cheese

Taleggio comes from Val Taleggio province in Bergamo and is a soft cheese made from whole cow's milk. It comes with an orangey skin which you remove before using.

1 Cut the peppers in half through the stalks and remove the seeds. Boil the pepper halves in hot water for 4 minutes and drain. Arrange the pepper halves on a baking tray, season and drizzle with the olive oil.

2 Cook the rice according to packet instructions, drain and leave to cool.

3 Preheat the oven to 180°C/fan oven 160°C/Gas Mark 4. Add the Taleggio, mascarpone, pistachios and spring onions to the rice and mix well. Spoon the rice mixture into the peppers, sprinkle with the grated Parmesan and cook in the oven for 20 minutes. Serve immediately.

roasted fennel and ricotta gratin

SERVES 4

2 fennel bulbs, thinly sliced
olive oil
salt and freshly ground
    black pepper
100 g (3½ oz) ricotta cheese
60 g (2½ oz) breadcrumbs
1 teaspoon finely chopped
    fresh tarragon
1 teaspoon finely chopped
    parsley
25 g (1 oz) butter

Roasting fennel brings out its lovely mellow, aniseedy flavour which combines so well with the saltiness of the ricotta.

1 Preheat the oven to 200°C/fan oven 180°C/Gas Mark 6. Arrange the fennel slices on a baking tray and toss with a little olive oil, salt and pepper, making sure all the fennel is coated. Cook for 45 minutes until the fennel is crisp, stirring occasionally to prevent it sticking to the tray.

2 Remove the fennel from the oven and add the ricotta, toss well and season to taste. Lower the oven temperature to 190°C/fan oven 170°C/Gas Mark 5. Divide the fennel mixture between 4 oiled ramekin dishes or 1 large dish.

3 In a small bowl, mix together the breadcrumbs, tarragon and parsley and sprinkle over the fennel. Dot with the butter and cook for 20 minutes until golden.

SUMMER lunch dishes

linguine with four-tomato sauce

SERVES 4

4 tablespoons olive oil

1 garlic clove, crushed

175 g (6 oz) plum tomatoes, skinned

175 g (6 oz) cherry tomatoes, skinned

100 g (3½ oz) sun-dried tomatoes, sliced

15 g (½ oz) bunch basil, torn into small pieces, plus extra to garnish

salt and freshly ground black pepper

400 g (13 oz) linguine

½ vegetable stock cube

500 ml (18 fl oz) hot water

1½ tablespoons tomato purée

60 g (2½ oz) Parmesan cheese, grated

If you don't have all the tomatoes for this simple dish just use what you do have, but make sure you have tomato purée as this holds the sauce together.

1 Heat the oil in a large, deep frying pan. Add the garlic, plum, cherry, and sun-dried tomatoes and basil. Cook over a low heat for 10 minutes – the tomatoes will soften so mash them gently with the back of a wooden spoon. Season the sauce to taste.

2 Meanwhile, cook the linguine in a large pan of boiling water according to packet instructions.

3 In a bowl, mix the stock cube with the hot water and add half of this to the tomato mixture. Cook for 15 minutes. Add the remaining stock and the tomato purée and cook for a further 15 minutes.

4 Add the drained pasta to the tomato sauce and cook for 1 minute. Divide between warmed serving plates and sprinkle with Parmesan and fresh basil.

pasta alla norma

SERVES 4

4 tablespoons olive oil

1 onion, cut into small cubes

2 garlic cloves, crushed

1 large aubergine, cut into
small cubes

1 small red pepper,
deseeded and cut into
small cubes

1 small yellow pepper,
deseeded and cut into
small cubes

2 small tomatoes, chopped

500 g (1 lb) trofie pasta or
pasta of your choice

4 tablespoons chopped
fresh basil

4 tablespoons chopped
fresh Italian parsley

125 g (4 oz) ricotta cheese,
crumbled

1 teaspoon salt

freshly ground black pepper

This easy-to-make rich, chunky sauce can also be served with a crisp salad but without the pasta.

1 Heat the oil in a pan and fry the onion, garlic, aubergine and peppers for 5 minutes. Add the tomatoes and cook for a further 5 minutes.

2 Cook the pasta according to the packet instructions.

3 Remove the sauce from the heat and add the basil, parsley, ricotta, salt and pepper. Drain the pasta, toss with the sauce and serve immediately.

Zilli know-how

Trofie pasta, from Liguria, is made only with flour and water and is rolled into small sausages and then twisted. It is difficult to find outside Italy but is easy to make even if it takes a while, and you can always get your kids to help!

goat's cheese crostini
with swiss chard

SERVES 2

1 yellow pepper

2 tablespoons extra virgin
  olive oil

4 slices wholegrain bread

400 g (13 oz) Swiss chard,
  chopped

2 garlic cloves, finely sliced

salt and ground pink
  peppercorns

65 g (2½ oz) soft goat's
  cheese

1 bunch fresh chives,
  chopped

1 teaspoon chopped fresh
  thyme

*This makes a really tasty light lunch.
I always keep some soft goat's cheese in the
fridge as it's so useful for a quick snack.*

1 Preheat the oven to 220°C/fan oven 200°C/Gas Mark 7.
Place the whole pepper on a baking tray, drizzle with
1 tablespoon of the olive oil and cook for about 30 minutes to
blacken. Remove the pepper from the oven and place it in a
plastic bag, tie the bag and leave to cool. When cool, remove
the pepper from the bag and slip off the blackened skin. Core
and deseed the pepper and then cut it into slices.

2 Toast the bread and set on one side. Heat the remaining oil
in a large pan and add the chard, garlic and seasoning. Sauté
until the chard wilts slightly.

3 In a bowl, mix together the goat's cheese, chives and thyme,
and season to taste. Spread the cheese mixture over the
toasted bread, add the peppers and top with the chard. Serve
the crostini immediately.

grilled vegetable terrine

SERVES 6

2 red peppers

2 courgettes, cut lengthways
  into 5 mm (¼ inch) slices

2 aubergines, cut
  lengthways into
  5 mm (¼ inch) slices

6 eggs

200 ml (7 fl oz) double cream

100 g (3½ oz) Parmesan
  cheese, grated

salt and freshly ground
  black pepper

I normally say substitute your favourite vegetable, however for this recipe it is best to use the ones I have chosen as otherwise your terrine may not come out properly.

1 Put the whole peppers on a baking tray and place under a hot grill for 15 minutes, turning occasionally, until charred. Remove and place them in a bowl, cover with clingfilm and leave to cool. When the peppers are cool, remove the skin. Core and deseed the peppers and then cut into quarters.

2 Grill the courgette and aubergine slices and peppers until nice and soft. In a bowl, beat the eggs and then add the cream, cheese and seasoning.

3 Preheat the oven to 150°C/fan oven 130°C/Gas Mark 3. Line a terrine or loaf tin with baking paper and add a layer of sliced aubergine, 4 tablespoons of the egg mixture and then a layer of sliced courgettes, more eggs and a layer of peppers. Continue until all the ingredients have been used. Bake the terrine in the oven for 40 minutes. Remove and leave to cool, then turn out the terrine and slice to serve.

quinoa-stuffed beef tomatoes

SERVES 6
Suitable for vegans

6 beef tomatoes
1 tablespoon finely chopped
    fresh basil
2 tablespoons finely
    chopped oregano
300 g (10 oz) quinoa,
    steamed
salt and freshly ground
    black pepper
6 tablespoons olive oil

This is one of those versatile dishes where you can add or take away ingredients, just make sure to add lots of herbs as quinoa on its own does not have a very strong flavour.

1 Preheat the oven to 200°C/fan oven 180°C/Gas Mark 6. Slice the tops off the tomatoes and keep them on one side. Using a spoon, scoop out the middle of the tomatoes and reserve the pulp.

2 Mix the tomato pulp with the herbs, cooked quinoa and plenty of seasoning. Place the tomatoes on a baking tray and spoon the filling into the tomatoes. Top each tomato with a tomato lid, drizzle over the olive oil and cook for 45 minutes. Serve at once.

Zilli know-how

Quinoa (pronounced 'keen-wah') is a south American grain with a mild, slightly nutty flavour. It can be used in dishes instead of rice, couscous or bulgur. Quinoa is high in protein and contains all eight of the essential amino acids, as well as magnesium and iron, so is good to include in a vegetarian diet. It's gluten-free too. Cook following the packet instructions.

orzotto verde

SERVES 4

300 g (10 oz) spinach

100 g (3½ oz) broccoli florets

2 tablespoons extra virgin
   olive oil

50 g (2 oz) butter

4 banana shallots, finely
   chopped

2 garlic cloves, crushed

325 g (11 oz) pearl barley

250 ml (8 fl oz) white wine

1.5 litres (2½ pints) hot
   vegetable stock

1 bunch fresh mint

salt and freshly ground
   black pepper

100 g (3½ oz) peas

3 tablespoons chopped
   fresh parsley

4 tablespoons freshly grated
   pecorino cheese

4 slices goat's cheese

This is a tasty risotto made with pearl barley instead of arborio or carnaroli rice. The main difference is it takes longer to cook.

1 Blanch the spinach, drain well, removing as much water as possible and blitz in a food processor. Blanch the broccoli.

2 Heat the oil and half the butter in a large, deep frying pan, add the shallots and fry gently for 5 minutes until soft. Stir in the garlic and cook for 1 minute until it starts to soften. Add the barley and stir until it is glistening with butter. Add the wine and cook until all the wine has been absorbed.

3 In a separate pan, bring the stock to a simmer, add the mint and simmer for 10 minutes. Remove the mint and discard.

4 Add a ladleful of hot stock to the barley and cook over a moderate heat for 3–5 minutes, stirring, until the liquid has been absorbed. Season. Continue adding the stock, a ladleful at a time. Ten minutes before the orzotto is cooked, add the spinach purée, broccoli and the peas, and then continue cooking, adding the stock a ladleful at a time.

5 When the orzotto is ready, remove from the heat and stir in the remaining butter, parsley and pecorino. The finished risotto should be quite fluffy but not soupy. Cover and leave to stand for 1 minute. Divide the orzotto between 4 heatproof dishes, lay a slice of goat's cheese on top of each and cook under a hot grill for 1 minute until the goat's cheese is golden and bubbling. Serve immediately.

spiced grilled courgettes

SERVES 4
Suitable for vegans

3 courgettes, sliced or
    halved lengthways
3 tablespoons olive oil
2 tablespoons chopped
    fresh oregano
2 garlic cloves, minced
1 tablespoon chopped fresh
    rosemary
1 tablespoon Italian dry
    chilli flakes
salt and freshly ground
    black pepper

A great diet recipe as courgettes are very low in calories and high in potassium, and vitamins A and C. Good as a quick summer snack or part of a buffet lunch.

1 Preheat the grill. Brush the courgettes with the olive oil. Sprinkle both sides of the courgettes with oregano, garlic, rosemary, chilli, salt and pepper.

2 Grill the courgettes for about 4 minutes on each side until tender, then serve.

aubergine cannelloni

SERVES 4

2 aubergines
300 g (10 oz) ricotta cheese
50 g (2 oz) Parmesan cheese,
  grated
150 g (5 oz) mozzarella
  cheese, finely diced
15 g (½ oz) fresh basil, torn
  into pieces, plus extra
  to garnish
salt and freshly ground
  black pepper
200 g (7 oz) cherry tomatoes
4 teaspoons extra virgin
  olive oil

One of my favourite dishes – rather than using pasta you use the aubergine as the 'cannelloni'. The cheese filling and the aubergine go really well together.

1 Cut the aubergines lengthways into 5 mm (¼ inch) thick slices and grill on both sides until soft.

2 In a bowl, mix the ricotta with half the Parmesan and the mozzarella. Add almost all the basil and seasoning.

3 Spread the ricotta mixture over each aubergine slice and roll up.

4 Preheat the oven to 180°C/fan oven 160°C/Gas Mark 4. Arrange the aubergine rolls in a buttered roasting tin and sprinkle with the rest of the grated Parmesan. Bake in the oven for 10 minutes.

5 Meanwhile, blend the cherry tomatoes with the olive oil and remaining basil leaves in a blender or food processor. Pour the sauce into a pan and heat through. Serve the cannelloni, sprinkled with the extra basil, with the tomato sauce.

thai green curry
with quinoa

SERVES 4
Suitable for vegans

FOR THE SPICE PASTE
1 teaspoon each cumin and coriander seeds
5 fresh green chillies, deseeded
2 shallots, chopped
2 garlic cloves, chopped
4 cm (1½ inch) piece fresh ginger, grated
2 lemongrass stalks, roughly chopped
¼ teaspoon ground turmeric
½ tablespoon palm sugar
handful coriander leaves

FOR THE VEGETABLES
2 tablespoons vegetable oil
2 x 400 ml cans coconut milk
1 courgette, thickly sliced
salt and freshly ground pepper
125 g (4 oz) asparagus, halved
100 g (3½ oz) green beans, topped and tailed
50 g (2 oz) mangetout
100 g (3½ oz) bok choi, sliced
10 fresh basil leaves, plus extra for garnish
fresh chillies, to serve
200 g (7 oz) quinoa, steamed
lime wedges, to serve

If you can't find palm sugar use brown or white granulated sugar. Keep tasting the paste as you may have to use slightly more or less sugar depending on the brand.

1 To make the spice paste, dry-fry the cumin and coriander seeds for a few minutes until fragrant, then grind in a mortar and pestle. Transfer to a blender or food processor and add the remaining paste ingredients. Blitz for 5 minutes until smooth and set aside.

2 Gently warm the vegetable oil in a large pan over a low heat. Add 40 g (1½ oz) of the spice paste and cook the mixture for 2 minutes, stirring. Add the coconut milk, bring to the boil and simmer for 5 minutes.

3 Toss the courgette slices in a little oil, season, and fry on a hot griddle for 2 minutes on each side. Add the courgettes to the curry mixture and cook for 6 minutes. Add the asparagus, beans, mangetout and bok choi, and cook for 3–4 minutes. Stir in the basil leaves. Serve the curry sprinkled with the extra basil and chillies with the steamed quinoa and lime wedges to squeeze over.

bulgur wheat salad
with mint and apricots

SERVES 4

150 g (5 oz) bulgur wheat
250 ml (8 fl oz) boiling water
juice of 2 lemons
juice of 2 limes
2 tablespoons extra virgin
  olive oil
1 tablespoon honey
salt and freshly ground
  black pepper
4 apricots, diced
200 g (7 oz) peeled yam, cut
  into pieces and steamed
1 bunch fresh mint, finely
  chopped

This salad is full of fresh flavours and the citrus dressing adds a real zing. All it needs is a glass of chilled white wine. Enjoy!

1 Combine the bulgur wheat and the boiling water in a large bowl and leave to stand for about 1 hour until all the water has been absorbed.

2 Pour the lemon and lime juices, olive oil and honey into a small jug. Whisk well and season to taste. Add the apricots, yam and mint to the bulgur and toss to combine. Pour over the dressing and stir well. Chill before serving.

Zilli know-how

Bulgur wheat are wheat grains that have been precooked, cut and 'cracked'. It has a nutty flavour as a result and works very well in soups, salads and stuffings.

quinoa with leeks and shiitake mushrooms

SERVES 4
Suitable for vegans

480 ml (17 fl oz) hot
  vegetable stock
240 ml (7½ fl oz) water
salt and freshly ground
  black pepper
285 g (9½ oz) quinoa,
  washed
3 tablespoons chopped
  flat-leaf parsley
1 tablespoon extra virgin
  olive oil
75 g (3oz) chopped walnuts
2 large leeks, thinly sliced
600 g (1 lb 4 oz) shiitake
  mushrooms, thinly sliced
1 large red pepper, deseeded
  and chopped
60 ml (2½ fl oz) white wine

Shiitake mushrooms have a subtle flavour and work well here with the walnuts and leeks in this satisfying supper.

1 Place the stock and water in a large pan with a pinch of salt. Bring to the boil, add the quinoa, then cover and reduce the heat. Cook for 15 minutes or until the liquid has been absorbed. Add the parsley, 2 teaspoons of the oil and a grinding of black pepper. Stir in the walnuts and remove from the heat. Keep covered.

2 Heat the remaining oil in a saucepan and cook the leeks for 6 minutes. Add the mushrooms, red pepper and wine, and cook for 2 minutes. Season to taste. Serve the quinoa with the leeks and mushrooms spooned over the top.

strawberry and lemon roulade

SERVES 6

FOR THE ROULADE
3 eggs, separated
175 g (6 oz) caster sugar
60 g (2½ oz) self-raising flour
grated zest of 2 lemons
icing sugar, for dusting

FOR THE FILLING
125 ml (4 fl oz) whipping cream
125 g (4 oz) mascarpone cheese
100 g (3½ oz) sliced strawberries or raspberries
icing sugar, for dusting

For a change, try orange instead of lemon zest and then add some chocolate to the filling (melt the chocolate and add to the cream before mixing with the mascarpone).

1 Preheat the oven to 200°C/fan oven 180°C/Gas Mark 6. Grease and line a 40 x 20 cm (16 x 8 in) Swiss roll tin or baking tray. In a large bowl, whisk the egg yolks and caster sugar until combined, then fold in the flour and lemon zest. In a separate bowl, beat the egg whites until stiff peaks form and fold them into the lemon mixture.

2 Pour the mixture into the lined tin and smooth with a palette knife. Cook for 8 minutes until golden. Remove the roulade from the oven and turn out onto a sheet of greaseproof paper dusted with icing sugar. Set on one side.

3 In a bowl, whip the cream and then fold in the mascarpone. Peel the lining paper off the roulade and spread over the cream. Arrange the sliced strawberries or raspberries over the cream and carefully roll up the roulade. Dust with icing sugar and serve cut into slices.

apricot and vanilla tartlets

SERVES 8

FOR THE PASTRY
220 g (7½ oz) plain flour,
    plus extra for dusting
1 teaspoon salt
150 g (5 oz) unsalted butter,
    cut into small pieces
7 tablespoons cold water

FOR THE FILLING
2 eggs, beaten
100 g (3½ oz) caster sugar
45 g (1½ oz) unsalted butter,
    melted
75 ml (3 fl oz) treacle
1 teaspoon vanilla extract
125 g (4 oz) ready-to-eat
    dried apricots, chopped
mascarpone cheese,
    to serve

Any firm fruit like peaches, nectarines or pears – or even a combination – will also work just as well for this dessert.

1 Preheat the oven to 160°C/fan oven 140°C/Gas Mark 3. Lightly grease 8 x 7cm (3 inch) round tart tins.

2 To make the pastry, sift together the flour and salt into a bowl. Add the butter and sprinkle a tablespoon of water over the mixture, gently mixing together with a fork. Continue adding the water, a little at a time, until the mixture comes together. Form the dough into a ball and turn onto a lightly floured work surface. Roll out the pastry and cut out 8 x 13 cm (5 inch) circles. Fit the pastry circles into the greased tart tins.

3 In a large bowl, combine the eggs, sugar, melted butter, treacle, and vanilla extract. Mix well and then stir in the apricots. Pour an equal amount of apricot mixture into each pastry-lined tart tin.

4 Bake the tartlets in the preheated oven for 30–35 minutes until the pastry is golden brown and the filling is set. Serve warm with dollops of mascarpone.

cherry and vecchia romagna fritters

SERVES 4

200 g (7 oz) plain flour
pinch of salt
50 g (2 oz) caster sugar
1 teaspoon baking powder
75 ml (3 fl oz) milk
2 tablespoons Vecchia
   Romagna brandy
1 egg
175 g (6 oz) cherries, stoned
   and chopped
vegetable oil, for deep frying
icing sugar, for dusting

If you are making this for your children, you can omit the brandy and increase the amount of milk.

1 Sift the flour, salt, sugar and baking powder into a bowl. In a separate bowl, beat together the milk, brandy and egg. Pour the milk mixture into the flour and beat to form a smooth batter. Fold in the cherries.

2 Heat the oil in a fryng pan and drop spoonfuls of the cherry batter into the hot oil and fry for 2–3 minutes until golden brown. Remove, drain on kitchen paper and keep warm. Repeat with the remaining batter. Dust the fritters with icing sugar and serve warm.

Zilli know-how

Distilled from trebbiano grapes, **Vecchia Romagna** is the biggest Italian brandy export. It is aged for three years in oak casks and has a strong, dry, aromatic flavour with a warm colour.

peach, walnut and brandy brûlée

SERVES 4

8 egg yolks
100 g (3½ oz) caster sugar
500 ml (18 fl oz) double
  cream
1 vanilla pod, split and seeds
  extracted
1 tablespoon brandy
100 g (3½ oz) walnuts,
  chopped
1 peach, stoned and diced
2 tablespoons demerara
  sugar

Everyone is always a bit wary of brûlées but they are easy to make as long as you cook them in a bain-marie in the oven. Besides, the best bit is blowtorching at the end!

1 Preheat the oven to 150°C/fan oven 130°C/Gas Mark 2. In a bowl, beat together the egg yolks and caster sugar until pale. Pour the cream into a pan, add the vanilla pod and seeds, and bring to the boil. Remove the vanilla pod and whisk the hot cream into the egg mixture. Stir in the brandy.

2 Pour the mixture into 4 ramekins and place in a roasting tin with enough hot water to come halfway up the sides of the ramekins. Add a few walnut pieces and peaches to the top of each ramekin and cook for 40 minutes until just set.

3 Remove the ramekins from the oven and tin and set aside to cool. When cold, chill the puddings for 2 hours. Sprinkle over the demerara sugar and place under a hot grill for 2 minutes until bubbling and melted (or use a blowtorch to caramelise the top). Chill before serving.

italian summer pudding

SERVES 6

6 tablespoons freshly
squeezed orange juice

3 tablespoons Grand
Marnier

30 sponge fingers
(preferably Pavesini
biscuits available from
most Italian delis)

6 eggs, separated

165 g (5½ oz) caster sugar

325 ml (11 fl oz) double
cream

500 g (1 lb) mascarpone
cheese

2 tablespoons vanilla extract

250 g (9 oz) strawberries,
sliced

3 tablespoons icing sugar

This tiramisu-type pud is normally made with coffee. I prefer this lighter version and the orange and strawberries make it a lovely summer pudding.

1 Mix together the orange juice and Grand Marnier. Dip half the sponge fingers quickly in the mixture, do not allow to soak, then lay on the bottom of a square flat dish.

2 In a heatproof bowl over a pan of simmering water, whisk the egg yolks and caster sugar. Remove from the heat and beat until pale, doubled in volume and creamy.

3 In a separate bowl, whisk the egg whites until stiff. In a large bowl, beat the cream until thick. Fold the mascarpone into the cream, then fold in the egg whites and vanilla extract. Finally, fold in the egg yolk mixture.

4 Spread some of the creamy mixture over the soaked sponge fingers in the dish then add a layer of strawberries. Dip the remaining sponge fingers in the orange juice mixture. Continue layering the sponge fingers, creamy mixture and strawberries, ending with sponge fingers. Cover with cling film and chill for 2 hours.

5 Remove the cling film and then completely cover the top of the summer pudding with icing sugar and serve.

Zilli know-how

Pavesini biscuits are light, sweet biscuits which melt in the mouth. They are made with flour, sugar and fresh eggs with no added fat and are only 8 calories each.

autumn

This season's stars include mushrooms,
squash, apples and pears — an
autumn harvest not to be missed.

coconut and coriander soup
with sweet potato

SERVES 6

1 tablespoon olive oil

1 tablespoon butter

1 onion, sliced

2 garlic cloves, crushed

500 g (1 lb) sweet potatoes,
  peeled and diced

600 ml (1 pint) hot vegetable
  stock

400 ml can coconut milk

1 bunch coriander, chopped,
  plus extra to garnish

salt and freshly ground
  black pepper

red chilli slices, to garnish

crusty bread, to serve

This is a lovely warming soup for those days when it is cold and brisk; the coconut milk makes it light but tasty.

1 Heat the oil and butter in a large pan and fry the onion and garlic for 5 minutes over a medium heat until the onion is soft and golden.

2 Add the potatoes to the pan and cook for 5 minutes, then add the stock and stir in the coconut milk. Cook for 20 minutes until the potatoes are soft. Remove the pan from the heat.

3 Blitz the soup in a blender or food processor with the coriander. Heat through if necessary, and season to taste. Serve the soup in warmed bowls, sprinkled with chilli slices and coriander, with crusty bread.

spicy falafel
with mint yogurt

SERVES 5

FOR THE FALAFEL

250 g (8 oz) dried fava beans, soaked overnight

½ bunch coriander, chopped

½ bunch parsley, chopped

50 g (2 oz) bulgur wheat, soaked in hot water for 10 minutes

1 tablespoon ground cumin

½ tablespoon ground coriander

½ tablespoon paprika

½ tablespoon cayenne

1 tablespoon garlic purée

½ tablespoon bicarbonate of soda

salt and freshly ground black pepper

vegetable oil, for frying

FOR THE MINT YOGURT

200 ml (7 fl oz) Greek yogurt

50 g (2 oz) chopped fresh mint

salt and freshly ground black pepper

TO SERVE

pitta breads

sliced tomatoes, red onion and cucumber

Falafel is a Middle Eastern dish usually made with chickpeas. I've used a mixture of beans and bulgur wheat here, which I find works better.

1 Put the beans in a large pan and cover with water. Bring to the boil and boil for 10 minutes, add a little salt and simmer for about 1 hour until soft.

2 To make the mint yogurt, mix the yogurt, mint and seasoning together in a small bowl and set on one side.

3 Drain the beans and put in a blender or food processor. Add all the remaining falafel ingredients and blend to a smooth paste. Shape the mixture into little 'meatballs'.

4 Heat the oil and deep-fry the falafel for about 3 minutes until golden brown. Drain on kitchen paper and serve warm in pitta breads with some sliced tomatoes, red onion and cucumber, and a dollop of the mint yogurt.

chanterelle and tarragon crostone

2 tablespoons olive oil

300 g (10 oz) chanterelle
  mushrooms, brushed
  not washed

salt and freshly ground
  black pepper

1 garlic clove, chopped

½ bunch tarragon, leaves
  stripped

175 ml (6 fl oz) dry white
  wine

1 tablespoon butter

4 x 1 cm (½ inch) thick slices
  white bread

The mild peppery taste of the chanterelles
makes this dish, ordinary mushrooms
just would not cut it so try to get hold of
chanterelles, or you could use ceps instead.

1 Heat the oil in a pan and, when very hot, add the
mushrooms and seasoning. Cook for 2 minutes and add the
garlic, tarragon leaves and wine. Cook the mushrooms for a
further 5 minutes, then add the butter. Remove from the heat.

2 Toast the bread, spoon over the mushroom mixture and
serve immediately.

tofu skewers
and butter bean pâté

SERVES 5
Suitable for vegans

FOR THE SKEWERS
**1 red pepper, halved
    and deseeded
1 yellow pepper, halved
    and deseeded
1 green pepper, halved
    and deseeded
1 aubergine
1 red onion
400 g (13 oz) tofu
2 courgettes
10 cherry tomatoes
10 button mushrooms
olive oil, for brushing**

FOR THE PATE
**250 g (8 oz) dried butter
    beans, soaked overnight
    or 2 x 410 g cans butter
    beans, rinsed and drained
salt and freshly ground
    black pepper
2 tablespoons olive oil
1 tablespoon chopped fresh
    rosemary
1 garlic clove, crushed
½ chilli, deseeded and
    sliced**

Dried butter beans are available from health food shops or use the canned variety or chickpeas if you prefer. Any leftover pâté is great the next day on toast.

1 Cut the peppers, aubergine, onion and tofu into large cubes. Peel the courgettes into ribbons and wrap a courgette ribbon around each cherry tomato. Thread all the vegetables and tofu alternately on to 10 x 25 cm (10 inch) skewers.

2 To make the pâté, rinse the dried butter beans, put them into a large pan and cover with water. Bring to the boil and boil for 10 minutes then add a little salt and simmer for about 1 hour until soft. Drain and blitz in a blender or food processor with the remaining ingredients (be careful how much salt you add as the water the beans were cooked in was salted). If you are using canned beans, simply add them to the blender or food processor with the rest of the pâté ingredients.

3 Preheat the oven to 180°C/fan oven 160°C/Gas Mark 4. Line a baking tray with foil, lay the skewers on the tray and drizzle with oil. Cook the skewers for 20 minutes, turning them occasionally. Serve with the butter bean pâté.

Zilli know-how

Tofu is well known for its nutritional values and its versatility. Made from soya milk, it is a soft cheese-like food, which on its own is quite bland, but it has the benefit of absorbing the flavours of other ingredients very well, making it perfect for vegetarian cooking.

cavolo nero involtini
with paprika dressing

SERVES 4
Suitable for vegans

FOR THE DRESSING
1 tablespoon smoked paprika
100 ml (3½ fl oz) extra virgin olive oil

FOR THE PARCELS
4 tablespoons olive oil
1 shallot, chopped
2 garlic cloves, chopped
2 tablespoons chopped fresh lemon thyme
1 red chilli, deseeded and chopped
500 g (1 lb) firm tofu, crushed with your hand
100 g (3½ oz) cooked spinach
salt and freshly ground black pepper
1 head cavolo nero

These little cabbage parcels are filled with a tofu, spinach and lemon thyme mixture and make a superb starter.

1 To make the dressing, blend together the paprika and oil with a little salt and set aside.

2 To make the parcels, heat the oil in a pan and fry the shallot, garlic, thyme and chilli for 5 minutes over a low heat. Add the tofu and spinach, mix well and cook for a further 10 minutes. Add seasoning to taste. Blend the tofu mixture in a blender or food processor.

3 Remove the stalks from the cavolo nero and cook the leaves in boiling salted water for 5 minutes. Drain and submerge the leaves in iced water to stop them cooking further. Drain and pat dry with kitchen paper.

4 Take one leaf, add a teaspoon of the tofu mixture and wrap the leaf around the filling. Serve the involtini at room temperature or cold, drizzled with some of the dressing.

Zilli know-how

A loose-leafed cabbage from Italy, **cavolo nero** translates as 'black cabbage' although it is a deep green colour. It has a pleasant, slightly bitter flavour. You can use kale or Savoy cabbage in its place, if you prefer.

coriander hummus
and bread sticks

SERVES 4
Suitable for vegans

1 aubergine
410 g can chickpeas, rinsed
   and drained
3 garlic cloves, chopped
½ red chilli, deseeded and
   chopped
1 bunch coriander
6 tablespoons extra virgin
   olive oil
salt and freshly ground
   black pepper
bread sticks, to serve

As a snack, nothing beats hummus and pitta bread, and the addition of coriander and chilli really lifts this version.

1 Preheat the oven to 180°C/fan oven 160°C/Gas Mark 4. Prick the aubergine all over with a fork, place it on a baking tray and roast in the oven for about 20 minutes until soft.

2 Cut the aubergine in half lengthways and scoop out the flesh into a food processor. Add the chickpeas, garlic, chilli and coriander, and blitz for 1 minute. Then, with the machine running, slowly add the olive oil in a steady stream. Season the hummus, transfer to a bowl and serve with bread sticks.

Zilli know-how

Sprinkle the top of the hummus with paprika and drizzle with extra virgin olive oil if you're serving this to your friends at a dinner party.

orecchiette with mushrooms

SERVES 4

2 tablespoons olive oil

250 g (8 oz) chiodini mushrooms (you can also use chanterelle or small fresh porcini)

1 garlic clove, chopped

salt and freshly ground black pepper

100 ml (3½ fl oz) white wine

100 ml (3½ fl oz) hot vegetable stock

2 tablespoons chopped fresh parsley

125 ml (4 fl oz) double cream

500 g (1 lb) orecchiette pasta

3 tablespoons freshly grated Parmesan cheese

Orecchiette means 'little ears' in Italian and this is what this pasta looks like. You can use another short pasta if you cannot find it.

1 Heat the oil in a pan and, when very hot, add the mushrooms and garlic, and sauté until golden. Season and add the wine. Reduce for 2 minutes and then add the stock, parsley and cream.

2 Meanwhile, cook the pasta according to packet instructions.

3 Drain the pasta and add to the mushrooms, cook for a further minute, tossing to ensure the sauce coats the pasta. Serve with fresh Parmesan.

Zilli know-how

Chiodini mushrooms look like the top of a nail, hence the name, which means little nail. They cannot be cultivated so you will only find wild chiodini.

truffle and parmesan soufflés

2 tablespoons butter, plus
    extra for greasing
4 tablespoons breadcrumbs
4 tablespoons plain flour
75 ml (3 fl oz) milk
200 g (7 oz) mozzarella
    cheese, cut into pieces
2 tablespoons freshly grated
    Parmesan cheese
salt and freshly ground
    black pepper
50 g (2 oz) fresh truffle,
    finely sliced, or use truffle
    paste
4 eggs, separated
4 tablespoons truffle oil,
    to drizzle

The trick to making soufflés is not to panic! This recipe is very simple, just make sure to whisk the egg whites properly and fold them in gently so they don't lose all the air.

1 Preheat the oven to 190°C/fan oven 170°C/Gas Mark 5. Butter 4 ramekins and coat with the breadcrumbs.

2 Mix together the flour and milk. Melt the butter in a pan and gradually stir in the milk mixture. Continue stirring and cooking the sauce until it just reaches boiling point. Cook the sauce for 3 minutes, then add the mozzarella, Parmesan, seasoning, truffle and egg yolks.

3 In a large bowl, whisk the egg whites to stiff peaks. Gently fold the whites into the truffle mixture. Pour into the coated ramekins and cook for 23 minutes. Serve the soufflés immediately with some truffle oil drizzled on top.

gnocchi with aubergine and tomato sauce

SERVES 4

FOR THE SAUCE

**1 aubergine, peeled and
    cut into cubes**

**salt and freshly ground
    black pepper**

4 tablespoons olive oil

**1 small onion, finely
    chopped**

1 garlic clove, crushed

400 g can chopped tomatoes

**1 bunch fresh basil, torn
    into pieces**

2 bay leaves

FOR THE GNOCCHI

**1 kg (2 lb) large floury
    potatoes, such as
    King Edwards**

salt

2 egg yolks

**200 g (7 oz) plain flour,
    plus extra for rolling**

**1 litre (1¾ pints) water
    or vegetable stock,
    for poaching**

Making gnocchi is easy, so I'm not sure why I don't make them more often!

1 Place the aubergine in a colander, sprinkle with salt and leave for about 1 hour to remove the excess water. Rinse, drain and dry the aubergine. Heat 1 tablespoon of the oil in a pan and fry the aubergine for 2–3 minutes to seal. Remove from the pan and set on one side.

2 Heat the remaining oil in a large deep pan, add the onion and cook over a very low heat for 5 minutes until soft but not brown. Stir in the garlic, tomatoes and basil. Add the bay leaves and cook over a low heat for 15 minutes. Add the aubergine to the sauce and cook for another 15 minutes until the sauce is very thick. Season well and keep warm.

3 Meanwhile, cook the unpeeled potatoes in a pan of boiling salted water for 30 minutes until soft. Drain and allow to cool enough for you to handle. Peel the potatoes and mash or press through a potato ricer into a bowl. Season the potatoes with salt, then beat in the egg yolks and flour, a little at a time, to form a smooth, slightly sticky dough.

4 Tip out the dough onto a well-floured board, roll into long sausages about 1 cm (½ inch) thick and cut into sections about 2 cm (¾ inch) long. Place each piece on a fork, press down with your thumb and roll onto the board, leaving grooves on one side of the gnocchi.

5 In a large pan, bring the water or stock to the boil and add the gnocchi, about 40 at a time, and cook until they rise to the surface. Then cook for another 50–60 seconds. Remove with a slotted spoon to a large bowl and keep warm while cooking the remaining gnocchi.

6 Add the cooked gnocchi to the sauce, along with a little of the cooking water. Cook for 2 minutes and serve.

rigatoni with dolcelatte and truffle

SERVES 4

75 g (3 oz) unsalted butter
100 g (3½ oz) frozen peas
175 ml (6 fl oz) hot vegetable
   stock
250 g (8 oz) dolcelatte
   cheese, cut into pieces
75 g (3 oz) mascarpone
   cheese
400 g (13 oz) rigatoni pasta
100 g (3½ oz) rocket
10 g (½ oz) truffle paste
salt and freshly ground
   black pepper
freshly grated Parmesan
   cheese, to serve

A little truffle paste lifts this pasta dish from the ordinary to the extra special and it's so quick to put together.

1 Heat the butter in a pan until melted, add the peas and cook for 3 minutes. Add the stock and cook for a further 2 minutes. Stir in the dolcelatte and mascarpone, and remove from heat.

2 Cook the pasta according to the packet instructions.

3 Drain the pasta and add to the cheese mixture. Return the pan to the heat and toss the pasta and sauce to combine. Add the rocket and truffle paste, and cook for a further 2 minutes. Season and serve with the Parmesan.

Zilli know-how

Truffles are rare, edible mushrooms that are only harvested wild, and as a result, are very expensive. They are one of my favourite ingredients as they come from my home region of Abruzzo. I have been truffle-hunting with my cookery school, which was great fun! Truffle-hunting is big business and they used to use female pigs but they were difficult to control once the truffle was located, so now they have specially trained dogs, called Lagotto.

Truffle paste is cheaper to buy than whole truffles as it is usually made from the smaller, damaged truffles.

camembert and chard piadina

SERVES 4

50 g (2 oz) butter
2 tablespoons olive oil
1 shallot, finely chopped
2 bunches Swiss chard,
   sliced into strips
salt and freshly ground
   black pepper
1 teaspoon ground nutmeg
150 g (5 oz) Camembert,
   cut into pieces
4 piadina flatbreads
oil, for frying

Piadina is basically a flat piece of bread that looks like a tortilla that you fill and then roll, perfect for a quick easy lunch.

1 Heat the butter and oil in a pan, add the shallot and cook for 1 minute. Add the chard and cook for 10 minutes until soft and tender. Season and add the nutmeg. Remove from the heat, place in a colander and leave to drain.

2 When the chard has drained, transfer it to a bowl. Add the Camembert to the bowl and mix together.

3 Place the flatbreads on a board, divide the filling between them and roll up. Heat a little oil in a pan and fry the rolls until golden, or cook at 180°C/fan oven 160°C/Gas Mark 4 for 5 minutes. Serve with a salad or eat as a snack.

leek, chickpea and saffron pie

SERVES 5

1 tablespoon butter

1 tablespoon olive oil, plus
   extra for brushing

1 white onion, chopped

1 tablespoon chopped garlic

1 tablespoon chopped fresh
   sage

1 tablespoon chopped fresh
   thyme

1 tablespoon chopped fresh
   rosemary

100 ml (3½ fl oz) white wine

1 kg (2 lb) leeks, sliced

400 g can chickpeas, rinsed
   and drained

1 teaspoon saffron strands,
   steeped in a little warm
   water

salt and freshly ground
   black pepper

250 g ready rolled puff
   pastry sheets

Make this hearty pie when it starts getting cold. It is a wonderfully comforting dish with a lot of flavour, which the family will enjoy.

1 Melt the butter and oil in a large pan, add the onion, garlic, sage, thyme and rosemary, and cook for 3 minutes. Add the white wine and leeks. Cover the pan and cook for 15 minutes until the leeks are soft.

2 Stir in the drained chickpeas and saffron and cook for a further 3 minutes. Remove from the heat and season.

3 Preheat the oven to 220°C/fan oven 200°C/Gas Mark 7. Line a pie dish with some of the pastry, spoon in the filling and then cover with the remaining pastry. Use a fork to seal the edges. Brush the top of the pie with a little oil and bake for 15 minutes until golden.

barley and lentil vegetable risotto

SERVES 4

Suitable for vegans

1 tablespoon olive oil

2 leeks, sliced

1 garlic clove, crushed

1 carrot, diced

1 stick celery, diced

1 yellow pepper, deseeded
   and diced

1 sprig rosemary

1 sprig thyme

175 g (6 oz) puy lentils

175 g (6 oz) pearl barley

175 ml (6 fl oz) white wine

500 ml (18 fl oz) hot
   vegetable stock

100 g (3½ oz) frozen peas

100 g (3½ oz) spinach,
   chopped

Parmesan cheese shavings,
   to serve

This dish is full of great ingredients and makes a terrific lunch to give you lots of energy for the rest of the day.

1 Heat the oil in a large pan, add the leeks, garlic, carrot and celery and cook for 4 minutes. Stir in the yellow pepper and herbs. Cook for a further 1 minute, then add the lentils and pearl barley. Add the wine and cook until it has been absorbed. Add the stock, a ladleful at a time, stirring frequently. Continue adding the stock until the lentils and barley are nearly cooked.

2 Add the peas and spinach, and cook for a further 5 minutes. Serve topped with Parmesan shavings.

vegetable and pancake parcels

SERVES 6

FOR THE PANCAKES
250 g (8 oz) plain flour
2 eggs, beaten
250 ml (8 fl oz) milk
50 g (2 oz) butter, melted
salt and freshly ground
**   black pepper**
vegetable oil, for frying

FOR THE FILLING
100 ml (3½ fl oz) olive oil
1 garlic clove, crushed
500 g (1 lb) button
**   mushrooms, sliced**
200 g (7 oz) frozen peas
2 red peppers, roasted to
**   remove skins, deseeded**
**   and diced**
200 g (7 oz) cream cheese
4 tablespoons chopped
**   fresh parsley**

This is an ideal dinner party dish as it can be prepared ahead and finished when guests arrive, which means more time being a host and less time slaving in the kitchen!

1 To make the pancakes, sift the flour into a bowl. Add the eggs and beat together, then add the milk, melted butter and seasoning and beat well again. Heat a little oil in a 23–25 cm (9–10 inch) non-stick frying pan. Pour a sixth of the batter into the pan, swirling it around. Cook for 1–2 minutes until the batter is set and golden on the base. Flip over and cook for a further 1–2 minutes until golden on the other side. Repeat to make 6 pancakes in all. Set on one side and keep warm.

2 To make the filling, heat the oil in a pan, add the garlic, mushrooms and peas and cook for 2 minutes. Add the peppers, cook for 1 minute and remove from the heat. Stir in the cream cheese and parsley.

3 Preheat the oven to 180°C/fan oven 160°C/Gas Mark 4. Lay each pancake in a buttered ramekin. Spoon in the filling and fold over the pancakes to make the parcels.

4 Cook the ramekins for 15–20 minutes. Remove from the oven and turn out onto serving plates. Serve with some tomato sauce or béchamel sauce (see Pancake lasagne on page 32).

aubergine cordon bleu

SERVES 6

1 mozzarella cheese ball,
   cut into small cubes
½ bunch basil, chopped
1 plum tomato, cut into
   small cubes
salt and freshly ground
   black pepper
2 large aubergines
200 g (7 oz) plain flour
2 eggs, beaten
500 g (1 lb) breadcrumbs
sunflower oil, for frying
tomato salsa, to serve

While not the healthiest of dishes, this is certainly a very tasty and quick dinner when you are in a hurry.

1 In a bowl, mix together the mozzarella, basil, tomato and seasoning to taste.

2 Slice the aubergines into 1 cm (½ inch) thick rounds. Lay in a colander, sprinkle with salt, and leave to rest for 20 minutes. Rinse, drain and pat dry with kitchen paper.

3 Lay 1 slice of aubergine on a board and spoon over some of the mozzarella mixture. Cover with another slice of aubergine and press the edges together to form a 'sandwich'. Dust both sides in flour, dip in the eggs and then the breadcrumbs. Repeat the coating so that you have a double layer of breadcrumbs. Coat the remaining aubergine slices in the same way.

4 Either deep-fry the aubergine sandwiches or pan-fry in sunflower oil until golden. Serve hot with some tomato salsa.

bulgur crusted tofu

SERVES 4

500 g (1 lb) bulgur wheat

50 g (2 oz) butter, melted

100 g (3½ oz) fresh parsley, chopped

2 tablespoons chopped fresh mint

1 tablespoon chopped fresh rosemary

1 tablespoon chopped fresh sage

4 tablespoons olive oil

salt and freshly ground black pepper

500 g (1 lb) firm tofu, cut into 4 slices

200 g (7 oz) plain flour

2 eggs, beaten

oil, for frying

The crust on the tofu gives a lovely crispy outside to it. You can serve this with a spicy tomato sauce to add extra flavour.

1 Place the bulgur wheat in a bowl, cover with boiling water and stir in the butter. Leave the bulgur for 1 hour to absorb the water, then mix in the chopped parsley, mint, rosemary, sage, olive oil and seasoning.

2 Dip each slice of tofu in the flour, then in the eggs and finally in the bulgur mix, pressing it on well to ensure each slice is well coated.

3 Heat a little oil in a frying pan and cook the tofu slices for 2 minutes on each side until golden. Serve with Thai-style grilled vegetables, page 65.

soya bolognese and orecchiette

SERVES 6
Suitable for vegans

100 ml (3½ fl oz) extra virgin
  olive oil
1 shallot, finely chopped
2 garlic cloves, finely
  chopped
1 carrot, finely chopped
1 celery stick, finely
  chopped
1 tablespoon finely chopped
  fresh rosemary
1 tablespoon finely chopped
  fresh sage
1 tablespoon finely chopped
  thyme
500 g (1 lb) soya mince,
  rehydrated following
  packet instructions
100 ml (3½ fl oz) red wine
2 x 400 g cans chopped
  tomatoes
1 tablespoon tomato purée
400 g (13 oz) orecchiette
  pasta
freshly grated Parmesan
  cheese and basil sprigs,
  to serve

You need a lot of herbs here to make the flavours work as soya mince is quite bland. Make this for your non-vegetarian friends and they will be very happy!

1 Heat the oil in a pan and cook the shallot, garlic, carrot and celery over a medium heat for 10 minutes. Add all the herbs and cook for 5 more minutes.

2 Add the soya mince and wine, and reduce for 5 minutes. Add the tomatoes and tomato purée, and cook over a low heat for 20 minutes.

3 Cook the pasta according to packet instructions. Drain and add to the bolognese sauce. Toss to combine and serve with some Parmesan and fresh basil.

rosemary and thyme mushroom parcel

SERVES 4
Suitable for vegans

8 large porcini or flat
   mushrooms, brushed
   but not washed

4 garlic cloves, sliced

1 tablespoon chopped fresh
   rosemary

1 tablespoon chopped fresh
   lemon thyme

4 tablespoons olive oil

salt and freshly ground
   black pepper

1 splash very dry white wine

I love mushrooms – all mushrooms. These meaty ones make me think of autumn, and the aroma of this dish is magic.

1 Preheat the oven to 200°C/fan oven 180°C/Gas Mark 6. Place the mushrooms on a foil-lined baking tray. In a small bowl, mix together the garlic and rosemary. Cut little holes in each of the mushrooms and fill with the garlic and rosemary.

2 Sprinkle over the lemon thyme, olive oil and seasoning. Drizzle over the white wine. Cover with foil to form a parcel and cook the mushrooms for 20 minutes. Remove from the oven and take directly to the table. Open the foil parcel in front of your guests so they can enjoy the lovely aroma.

Zilli know-how

When using any **wild mushrooms** you need to brush them to clean them. Use a clean nail brush if you have one to remove all the excess soil without damaging the mushrooms, which is what tends to happen with washing. Mushroom brushes are relatively inexpensive and can be bought from most kitchen shops.

large pasta shells with gruyère and vegetables

SERVES 4

FOR THE PESTO
35 g (1½ oz) basil leaves
2 tablespoons pine nuts,
**   toasted**
2 garlic cloves, chopped
250 ml (8 fl oz) extra virgin
**   olive oil**
25 g (1 oz) Parmesan cheese,
**   freshly grated**
75 g (3 oz) pecorino cheese,
**   freshly grated**
salt and freshly ground
**   black pepper**

FOR THE PASTA
1 aubergine, cut into 1 cm
**   (½ inch) rounds**
olive oil, for brushing
2 courgettes, sliced
1 yellow pepper
1 red pepper
1 green pepper
16 large pasta shells, or
**   other large pasta shapes**

FOR THE CHEESE SAUCE
50 g (2 oz) unsalted butter
50 g (2 oz) plain flour
300 ml (½ pint) milk
75 g (3 oz) gruyère cheese
pinch mustard powder
grated Parmesan cheese,
**   to serve**

There is a lot of work in this recipe but most of it can be done beforehand and put together at the last minute.

1 To make the pesto, blitz all the ingredients together in a food processor. (If keeping for a while, ensure that the pesto is covered with olive oil to keep its freshness.)

2 Put the aubergine rounds in a colander over a bowl and sprinkle with salt. Leave to stand for at least 1 hour (the salt removes the bitterness and the excess water). Rinse, drain off the water and pat dry with kitchen paper. Brush a griddle pan with olive oil and chargrill the aubergines over a high heat on both sides. Chargrill the courgettes in the same way.

3 Preheat the oven to 180°C/fan oven 160°C/Gas Mark 4. Roast the peppers for 30 minutes, continually turning them. Remove from the oven and immediately place in a plastic bag, tie the ends and leave to cool. When cool, peel the skin off the peppers; halve and remove the seeds, and set on one side.

4 Cook the pasta shells according to packet instructions until al dente. Remove and toss with olive oil and set on one side.

5 Roughly chop the peppers, courgettes and aubergines and mix with the pesto. Spoon the filling into the pasta shells.

6 Melt the butter in a small pan, add the flour, stir continuously and cook for 1 minute. Gradually add the milk, whisking all the time to make a smooth white sauce. Add the gruyère, mustard and seasoning and continue stirring until cheese has melted.

7 Increase the oven to 190°C/fan oven 170°C/Gas Mark 5. Spread some cheese sauce onto the bottom of a baking dish and then arrange the stuffed pasta shells on top. Pour over the remaining sauce, sprinkle with Parmesan and cook for 20 minutes until golden and bubbling. Serve immediately.

chestnut and chocolate soufflés

butter, for greasing
100 g bar good-quality dark
    chocolate (such as Green
    and Black's), broken into
    pieces
4 egg whites
25 g (1 oz) caster sugar
20 g (¾ oz) chestnuts,
    finely chopped
2 egg yolks

You can, of course, use another dark chocolate but make sure it still has the smoothness of flavour, otherwise your soufflé will be bitter.

1 Preheat the oven to 150°C/fan oven 130°C/Gas Mark 2. Grease 4 ramekin dishes with butter.

2 Bring a pan of water to the boil and rest a stainless steel bowl on the pan. Add the chocolate to the bowl and melt, stirring occasionally.

3 In a separate bowl, whisk the egg whites for 5 minutes. Gradually add the sugar and chestnuts, whisking until the mixture thickens and forms stiff peaks.

4 Remove the melted chocolate from the heat, add the egg yolks and combine well. Add a spoonful of egg white to the mixture and stir in. Then carefully fold the chocolate mixture into the egg whites using a stainless steel spoon, folding in a gentle motion. Do not stir or you will knock out the air. Spoon the mixture into the ramekins. Cook the soufflés for 25 minutes and serve immediately.

baked honey and ricotta cheesecake

SERVES 4

FOR THE SPONGE BASE
**butter and flour, for
    preparing tin**
75 g (3 oz) caster sugar
75 g (3 oz) butter, softened
2 eggs, separated
75 g (3 oz) plain flour, sifted
**4 tablespoons cornflour,
    sifted**
1 teaspoon baking powder
pinch of salt

FOR THE TOPPING
500 g (1 lb) ricotta cheese
5 eggs
**100 ml (3½ fl oz) manuka
    honey, warmed**
pinch of ground cinnamon
grated zest of 2 lemons
2 teaspoons Marsala wine

Don't worry if the top of the cheesecake cracks slightly as this is normal. For those of you with a sweet tooth, make a blackberry coulis to serve with this cheesecake.

1 Preheat the oven to 180°C/fan oven 160°C/Gas Mark 4. Grease and flour a 20 cm (8 inch) round springform pan or cake tin with a removable base.

2 To make the sponge base, whisk together the sugar, butter and egg yolks until light and creamy. Gradually add the flour, cornflour, baking powder and salt, beating continuously.

3 In a separate bowl, whisk the egg whites until very stiff, and then gently fold into the sponge mixture. Pour the mixture into the tin and bake for 25 minutes.

4 Push the ricotta through a sieve into a bowl. Separate 3 of the eggs. Add the 2 whole eggs to the egg yolks, with the warm honey, cinnamon, and lemon zest, and mix well.

5 Whisk the 3 egg whites until stiff and then fold in the Marsala. Fold the egg whites into the ricotta mixture.

6 When the sponge base is almost cooked, reduce the oven temperature to 150°C/fan oven 130°C/Gas Mark 2. Pour the ricotta mixture onto the base and cook for another 25 minutes. Allow the cheesecake to cool a little before removing from the tin to cool completely.

Zilli know-how

Distinctive-flavoured **manuka honey** only comes from New Zealand as the manuka bushes grow wild there. It is not an accredited medicine but is being used more and more both internally and externally.

tofu limoncello cheesecake

200 g (7 oz) digestive biscuits, crushed

75 g (3 oz) butter or margarine, melted

1 tablespoon agar agar

grated zest and juice of 1 lemon

250 ml (8 fl oz) limoncello liqueur

400 g (13 oz) firm tofu

400 g (13 oz) coconut cream

115 g (3½ oz) caster sugar

fresh berries or berry sauce, to serve

Make sure you use coconut cream, if you use milk this recipe will not set properly. The strong flavour of the limoncello gives this cheesecake a delicious lemony taste.

1 Mix together the crushed biscuits with the butter or margarine. Press the mixture into the base of a 20 cm (8 inch) round springform pan or cake tin with a removable base.

2 In a pan on a very low heat, dissolve the agar agar with the lemon juice and limoncello.

3 Put the tofu, coconut cream, lemon zest, sugar and agar agar mixture into a food processor and blend together.

4 Spoon the tofu mixture over the biscuit base and smooth the surface. Chill for 1 hour until set. Serve with fresh berries or a berry sauce.

Zilli know-how

Agar agar is a vegetarian form of gelatine and is made from seaweed. It is used as a gelling agent. Agar agar is used mainly in Japanese cooking but it is becoming more popular in vegetarian cooking.

apple pavlova

SERVES 8

FOR THE MERINGUE
**4 egg whites, at room
  temperature**
200 g (7 oz) caster sugar
1 teaspoon ground cinnamon
1 teaspoon lemon juice
1 teaspoon vanilla extract
1 tablespoon cornflour

FOR THE APPLE SAUCE
**16 apples, peeled, cored
  and quartered**
200 ml (7 fl oz) water
**200 g (7 oz) white caster
  sugar**
1 teaspoon ground cinnamon
pinch of nutmeg

TO DECORATE
whipped double cream
fresh apple slices

As we all know, this dessert is named after the famous ballerina. I prefer my meringue with apples as I find the dish too sweet with berries.

1 Preheat the oven to 140°C/fan oven 120°C/Gas Mark 1. Line a large baking sheet with baking paper. Put the egg whites in a stainless steel bowl and, using an electric mixer, whisk until the whites form soft peaks. In a separate bowl, mix together the sugar and cinnamon and add the sugar mixture slowly (1 tablespoon at a time) to the egg whites, beating well after each addition. Continue whisking the meringue mixture for about 10 minutes until very stiff and glossy. Fold in the lemon juice, vanilla extract and cornflour.

2 Spread the mixture into a rough 20cm (8 inch) circle on the baking sheet, making a slight dip in the middle to hold the apples. Bake for 1¼ hours. Turn off the oven and leave the meringue inside to cool.

3 Meanwhile, make the apple sauce. Place the apples and water in a large pan, bring to the boil and simmer for about 10 minutes. Add the sugar, cinnamon and nutmeg, and cook for a further 2–3 minutes until the sugar has dissolved and the apple sauce has thickened. Leave until cold.

4 Place the meringue on a serving plate and spoon in the apple sauce. Top with whipped cream and apple slices.

carrot and walnut cake

SERVES 8

225 g (7½ oz) muscovado
   sugar
175 ml (6 fl oz) vegetable oil
3 eggs
100 g (3½ oz) self-raising
   flour
1 teaspoon ground cinnamon
150 g (5 oz) carrots, grated
25 g (1 oz) walnuts, toasted
   and chopped
4 dried figs, chopped
Greek yogurt, to serve

A slice of this lovely cake is perfect with an espresso. Great comfort food when it starts to get rainy and cold!

1 Line a 20 cm (8 inch) round cake tin with greaseproof paper. Preheat the oven to 150°C/fan oven 130°C/Gas Mark 2.

2 In a mixing bowl, add the sugar and then whisk in the oil. Add the eggs and mix until smooth. Add the flour and cinnamon, and mix well, making sure the mixture is smooth with no lumps.

3 Add the grated carrots, walnuts and figs, and mix well. Pour into the cake tin and bake for 1 hour 20 minutes. Remove from the oven and leave to cool before removing from the cake tin. Serve with Greek yogurt.

winter

When it's cold outside, it's time to turn to warming comfort food — wonderful soups, casseroles and pies.

cannellini bean and rosemary soup

FOR THE PARMESAN CROUTES
4 slices French loaf, cut on the diagonal
1 tablespoon extra virgin olive oil
1 teaspoon sea salt
4 garlic cloves, halved
60 g (2½ oz) freshly grated Parmesan cheese
freshly ground black pepper

FOR THE SOUP
25 g (1 oz) unsalted butter
2 tablespoons olive oil, plus extra for drizzling
1 garlic clove
2 carrots, sliced
1 onion, finely chopped
2 stalks celery, diced
1 litre (1¾ pints) hot vegetable stock
2 x 410 g cans cannellini beans, rinsed and drained
2 tablespoons chopped fresh rosemary

This simple soup is one of my favourites. I think cannellini beans are underused in cooking and it is hard to see why as this dish is always popular with my friends.

1 Preheat the oven to 200°C/fan oven 180°C/Gas Mark 6. To make the Parmesan croûtes, place the bread on a tray, drizzle with the olive oil and sprinkle with sea salt. Bake the bread, turning occasionally, for 10–15 minutes until golden brown. Remove from the oven and rub the garlic over the bread while it is still hot, sprinkle the Parmesan and pepper on top of the bread and set on one side.

2 Meanwhile, make the soup. Heat the butter and oil in a pan. Add the garlic, carrots, onion and celery, and cook for 8 minutes until the onion is translucent and then remove the garlic. Add the vegetable stock and bring to the boil. Reduce the heat and cook for 20 minutes. Add the beans and rosemary and cook for a further 15 minutes.

3 Place half the soup in a blender or food processor and blitz until smooth, return to the remaining soup in the pan and reheat. Flash the croûtes under a hot grill until the cheese is golden. Pour the soup into warmed bowls and float the croûtes on top or serve them alongside. Drizzle with a little oil and serve immediately.

italian broth
with rustic pizza

FOR THE SOUP

1 courgette, roughly chopped

1 stick of celery, roughly chopped

1 carrot, roughly chopped

1 onion, roughly chopped

1 leek, roughly chopped

1 potato, roughly chopped

1 bay leaf

½ bunch parsley, stalks only

1.5 litres (2½ pints) hot vegetable stock

salt and freshly ground black pepper

FOR THE PIZZA

2 eggs, separated

2 tablespoons freshly grated Parmesan cheese

1 tablespoon chopped fresh parsley

1 teaspoon plain flour

pinch of baking powder

salt and freshly ground black pepper

As the nights start drawing in early around this time of year, this dish is great for lifting your spirits. Full of flavour and the pizza rustica just adds that bit extra.

1 To make the soup, place all the vegetables, herbs, stock and seasoning in a large pan and bring to the boil. Cook for 30 minutes until tender.

2 Meanwhile, make the pizza. Preheat the oven to 180°C/ fan oven 160°C/Gas Mark 4. Line a 10 x 15 cm (4 x 6 inch) roasting tin with baking paper. Whisk the egg whites until they form stiff peaks. In a separate bowl, mix the egg yolks, cheese, parsley, flour, baking powder and seasoning. Using a wooden spoon, fold the egg yolk mix into the egg white. Pour the mixture into the tin and cook for 10–15 minutes until the pizza is golden.

3 Strain the soup and return the broth to the heat to keep warm. Remove the pizza from the oven and turn upside down on a board. Remove the baking paper. Cut the pizza into small dice and sprinkle into 4 warmed soup bowls. Pour over the soup and serve immediately.

red onion and roquefort soup

SERVES 6

2 tablespoons butter
2 red onions, finely sliced
1 teaspoon finely chopped
   garlic
60 g (2½ oz) plain flour
½ teaspoon finely chopped
   fresh oregano
50 ml (2 fl oz) dry or sweet
   sherry
1.5 litres (2½ pints) hot
   vegetable stock
100 g (3½ oz) Roquefort
   cheese, chopped
500 ml (18 fl oz) single
   cream
salt and freshly ground
   black pepper

The trick to this recipe is to almost caramelise the onions so the sweetness cuts through the strong flavour of the Roquefort.

1 Melt the butter in a pan, add the onions and cook over a medium heat for 10 minutes. Add the garlic, flour and oregano, and cook for 2 minutes, stirring continuously. Add the sherry and carry on stirring. Add the stock and bring to the boil.

2 Reduce the heat and add the cheese, stirring until it has melted. Add the cream and cook for 2 minutes. Season the soup and serve.

figs with goat's cheese and pine nuts

SERVES 4

6 fresh figs, halved

60 g (2½ oz) pine nuts, toasted

200 g (7 oz) goat's cheese, cut into 12 pieces

2 tablespoons extra virgin olive oil

juice of 1 lemon

150 g (5 oz) watercress

I love fresh figs. The rich potassium contained in the fruit helps to maintain blood pressure and gives you an energy boost. All this and it tastes good!

1 Preheat the grill to hot. Place the figs on a baking tray and press the pine nuts into the figs. Place a piece of the cheese on top of each fig half. Grill for 4 minutes until the cheese is bubbling and golden brown.

2 Meanwhile, in a small bowl, whisk together the oil and lemon juice and dress the watercress. Place some watercress on each serving plate and arrange the figs on top.

swiss chard and artichoke tartlets

SERVES 6
Suitable for vegans

FOR THE PASTRY
125 g (4 oz) margarine
250 g (8 oz) plain flour
½ teaspoon salt
**1 tablespoon chopped fresh
    parsley**
100 ml (3½ fl oz) soya milk

FOR THE FILLING
**2 generous pinches of
    saffron strands**
600 g (1 lb 4 oz) firm tofu
1 tablespoon olive oil
1 onion, finely chopped
**1 tablespoon each chopped
    fresh thyme and sage**
**100 g (3½ oz) Swiss chard,
    sliced and cooked**

FOR THE SAUCE
1 tablespoon olive oil
1 onion, finely diced
4 garlic cloves, finely diced
**5–6 Jerusalem artichokes,
    peeled and sliced**
175 ml (6 fl oz) white wine
**salt and freshly ground
    black pepper**
**150 ml (¼ pint) hot
    vegetable stock**
**25 g (1 oz) chopped fresh
    parsley**

Although it seems like a lot of effort, I really like having these tarts as a starter or serve them with salad for a light lunch.

1 Preheat the oven to 180°C/fan oven 160°F/Gas Mark 4. To make the pastry, rub the fat into the flour and salt until the mixture resembles breadcrumbs. Add the parsley and bind together with the soya milk. Or whizz the pastry ingredients in a food processor. Roll out the dough and use to line 6 x 15cm (6 inch) tartlet cases. Cook in the oven for 15 minutes.

2 To make the filling, soak the saffron in a little water. Dice the tofu. Heat the oil in a pan and cook the onion, herbs and tofu for 2 minutes. Stir in the saffron and cook for a further 2 minutes. Season and add the chard. Roughly blend the mixture in a blender or food processor, then pipe or spoon into the tartlet cases and cook for 10 minutes.

3 While the tarts are cooking, make the sauce. Heat the oil in a pan and cook the onion and garlic for 1 minute. Add the artichokes, cook for 2 minutes and add the wine and seasoning. Once the wine has been absorbed, cover with the vegetable stock and cook for 20 minutes until the artichokes are soft. Stir in the parsley. Blitz the mixture in a blender or food processor, then sieve the sauce. Serve the tartlets immediately with the sauce spooned over.

Zilli know-how

Saffron is a very expensive spice but luckily you don't have to use a lot to get the flavour and colour you need. Saffron is from a flower and each stigma (from which we get the strands) is hand-picked – this costly labour is the reason for the high price.

squash gnocchi
with butter and sage sauce

SERVES 4

FOR THE GNOCCHI
**300 g (10 oz) butternut
    squash**
fresh sage leaves
olive oil
sea salt
**700 g (1 lb 7 oz) large floury
    potatoes, such as King
    Edwards**
2 egg yolks
**200 g (7 oz) plain flour, plus
    extra for rolling**
**2 litres (3½ pints) vegetable
    stock**

FOR THE SAUCE
6 tablespoons butter
10 sage leaves, chopped
juice of ½ lemon
**75 g (3 oz) freshly grated
    Parmesan cheese**

This is a good recipe to get your kids to help with as you can't go wrong and it isn't important what the gnocchi look like as long as you all had fun doing it!

1 Preheat the oven to 200°C/fan oven 180°C/Gas Mark 6. Peel the butternut squash and dice the flesh. Place the squash on a baking tray and scatter with sage, olive oil and sea salt. Cook for 30 minutes until tender. Remove the squash from the oven, discard the sage and press through a potato ricer into a bowl.

2 Meanwhile, cook the unpeeled potatoes in a large pan of boiling salted water for 30 minutes until soft. Drain and allow to cool slightly. When the potatoes are cool enough to handle, peel them and mash or press through a potato ricer into the same bowl as the squash. Season with salt then beat the egg yolks and flour into the potatoes and squash, a little at a time, to form a smooth, slightly sticky dough.

3 Tip the dough onto a well-floured board, then roll into long sausages about 1 cm (½ inch) thick. Cut into 2 cm (¾ inch) long sections with a spatula. Place each piece on a fork and press down with your thumb and roll onto the board, leaving grooves on one side of the gnocchi.

4 Heat the vegetable stock in a large pan and cook the gnocchi by dropping them, in batches, into the stock for about 5 minutes – when they float to the surface they are ready.

5 While your gnocchi are cooking, make the sauce. Melt the butter in a pan and heat gently until the butter becomes a light golden brown colour. Add the sage and remove from the heat, then add the lemon juice. Take the gnocchi from the stock and add to the sage sauce, adding a little of the stock as well. Toss together and then add the cheese. Toss again and serve immediately with extra cheese.

focaccia stuffed with mozzarella and red peppers

SERVES 4

2 red peppers
olive oil
sea salt and freshly ground
   black pepper
2 mozzarella cheese balls
1 tablespoon chopped fresh
   oregano
1 tablespoon chopped fresh
   parsley
100 ml (3½ fl oz) extra virgin
   olive oil
1 focaccia loaf

Bread is a major weakness of mine and there is nothing better than freshly made focaccia from the oven. This is the Italian equivalent of English cheese on toast.

1 Preheat the oven to 200°C/fan oven 180°C/Gas Mark 6. Place the whole peppers on a baking tray, drizzle with olive oil and sprinkle with salt. Cook for 30 minutes, turning occasionally. Remove the peppers from the oven, place in a bowl, cover with cling film and leave to cool. When cool, remove the skin and core and deseed the peppers. Cut the peppers into 5 cm (2 inch) strips.

2 Slice the mozzarella into 5 mm (¼ inch) thick pieces and put in a bowl. Add the roasted pepper strips, oregano, parsley, olive oil and seasoning.

3 Turn the oven temperature down to 180°C/fan oven 160°F/Gas Mark 4. Cut the focaccia in half horizontally. Spoon the mozzarella and pepper mixture over the bread base and pour over any remaining oil. Place the bread half on top and press down firmly. Cook the stuffed loaf for 15 minutes until the mozzarella has melted. Cut into 4 and serve immediately.

potato gratin

SERVES 4

olive oil
1 Spanish onion, finely
   sliced
1 garlic clove, halved
4 **King Edward potatoes,
   peeled and finely sliced**
200 g (7 oz) Cheddar cheese,
   grated
50 ml (2 fl oz) double cream
50 ml (2 fl oz) white wine
pinch of nutmeg
salt and freshly ground
   black pepper

You can use fontina cheese instead of Cheddar if you prefer, but however you look at this, the cream makes this dish very tasty but not for the calorie conscious.

1 Heat a little olive oil in a pan and cook the onion and garlic until soft. Remove from the heat and discard the garlic.

2 In a baking dish, place a layer of potatoes, then a layer of onions, then some cheese – use 150 g (5 oz) of the cheese in the layering process – and continue the layers finishing with sliced potatoes.

3 Preheat the oven to 180°C/fan oven 160°C/Gas Mark 4. In a bowl, mix together the cream, wine, nutmeg and seasoning, and pour over the potatoes. Sprinkle over the remaining cheese. Place a layer of baking paper on top of the dish and then wrap in foil. With a skewer, poke some holes in the foil and baking paper.

4 Cook the gratin for 1 hour 20 minutes. Check the potatoes are cooked, then remove the baking paper and foil and cook for a further 10 minutes until the top is golden.

fennel and radicchio salad
with blue cheese and pomegranate

SERVES 4

2 fennel bulbs

juice of 1 lemon

1 red radicchio

1 pomegranate

150 g (5 oz) blue cheese
    (dolcelatte or Stilton), cut
    into bite-sized pieces

100 g (3½ oz) mixed herb
    leaves

2 tablespoons walnut halves,
    toasted

FOR THE DRESSING

2 tablespoons extra virgin
    olive oil

2 teaspoons red wine
    vinegar

1 heaped teaspoon Dijon
    mustard

sea salt and freshly ground
    black pepper

I know it seems silly having a salad in the winter section, but this is a crisp, refreshing alternative to other winter dishes, and it gives you energy.

1 Slice the fennel, place in a bowl and add the lemon juice. Toss well to stop the fennel discolouring. Cut the radicchio into bite-sized pieces. Slice the pomegranate into quarters and remove the seeds.

2 To make the dressing, whisk together the olive oil, vinegar, mustard, sea salt and pepper.

3 Place the fennel, radicchio, pomegranate seeds, cheese, herb leaves and walnuts in a bowl. Add the dressing, toss well and serve.

Zilli know-how

Pomegranates are becoming easier to find in supermarkets now. You only eat the seeds of the pomegranate and discard everything else. The easiest way to remove the seeds is to tap them out with the back of a spoon as this avoids bruising or damaging the seeds.

root vegetable and red wine casserole

SERVES 4

Suitable for vegans

1 tablespoon olive oil, plus
    extra for drizzling
1 shallot, chopped
2 garlic cloves, finely
    chopped
1 celery stick, chopped
1 carrot, chopped
1 tablespoon finely chopped
    fresh rosemary
1 tablespoon finely chopped
    fresh sage
1 tablespoon finely chopped
    fresh thyme
2 beetroots, diced
1 parsnip, diced
1 swede, diced
200 g (7 oz) new potatoes,
    halved
400 g can chopped plum
    tomatoes
1 tablespoon tomato purée
175 ml (6 fl oz) good red wine
1 litre (1¾ pints) hot
    vegetable stock
boiled rice, to serve

Casseroles are normally made with meat or fish but I think this one made with vegetables is fabulous – go on, give it a go!

1 Heat the oil in a pan and cook the shallot, garlic, celery and carrot over a low heat for 5 minutes. Add the herbs and cook for a further 5 minutes.

2 Add the beetroots, parsnip, swede and potatoes and cook for a further 5 minutes. Add the tomatoes, tomato purée, wine and stock and cook for 30 minutes until the vegetables are all tender. Serve with rice and drizzle with a few drops of extra virgin olive oil before serving.

manuka honey glazed parsnips

SERVES 4

200 ml (7 fl oz) hot vegetable
    stock
4 parsnips, halved
    lengthways
salt and freshly ground
    black pepper
2 tablespoons manuka honey
2 tablespoons lemon juice
2 tablespoons butter

I like the sweetness of these parsnips and they are really good served with a nut roast. Or like me, you can just have them as a snack on their own.

1 Preheat the oven to 200°C/fan oven 180°C/Gas Mark 6. Pour the stock into a deep frying pan, add the parsnips with some salt and cook for 10 minutes until tender. Strain the parsnips, reserving the cooking liquid. Lay the parsnip halves on a baking tray.

2 Return the cooking liquid to the pan, add the honey, lemon juice and seasoning, bring to the boil and reduce by half. Pour the liquid over the parsnips, add the butter and toss to make sure the parsnips are well coated. Cook the parsnips in the oven for 20 minutes until golden brown and glazed.

parmesan risotto
in a parmesan basket

SERVES 4

FOR THE BASKET
**200 g (7 oz) Parmesan
   cheese, grated**

FOR THE CRANBERRY CONFIT
**100 ml (3½ fl oz) orange
   juice**
100 g (3½ oz) sugar
125 g (4 oz) fresh cranberries

FOR THE RISOTTO
2 tablespoons olive oil
50 g (2 oz) butter
1 shallot, finely chopped
1 teaspoon saffron threads
250 g (8 oz) arborio rice
200 ml (7 fl oz) white wine
**1.5 litres (2½ pints) hot
   vegetable stock**
**100 g (3½ oz) Parmesan
   cheese, grated**

The crunchiness of the cheesy basket here provides a texture contrast to the smoothness of the risotto.

1 Preheat the oven to 190°C/fan oven 170°C/Gas Mark 5. To make the baskets, place 4 round even piles of cheese on a large baking tray lined with baking parchment, spacing them well apart. Cook for a few minutes until melted, then remove from the oven and leave to cool a little. Turn a small bowl upside down and place a cheese disc over the top, gently pressing down the sides to form a basket. Repeat to make 4 baskets in total.

2 Pour the orange juice and sugar into a pan and bring to boil. Add the cranberries and cook for about 10 minutes until they are soft. Set on one side to cool and then chill until ready to use.

3 Heat the oil and half the butter in a large pan for 2 minutes. Add the shallot and saffron and cook for a further 3 minutes. Stir in the rice and cook for 4 minutes until the rice is well coated and transparent. Add the wine and cook for a few minutes until it has been absorbed. Add a ladleful of stock to the risotto, stirring well, and cook for 3–5 minutes until it has been absorbed. Continue to add the stock, a ladleful at a time, until all the stock has been absorbed and the risotto is tender and creamy. This should take about 20 minutes.

4 Remove the risotto from the heat and stir in the cheese and remaining butter. Place the cheese baskets on individual serving plates and fill with risotto. Top with a teaspoon of cranberry confit and serve.

grilled polenta

with slow-cooked tomatoes and mushrooms

SERVES 6

500 g (1 lb) plum tomatoes

salt and freshly ground
   black pepper

1 tablespoon chopped fresh
   oregano

100 ml (3½ fl oz) olive oil

500 g (1 lb) instant polenta

1 tablespoon butter, for
   greasing

2 teaspoons chopped garlic

500 g (1 lb) button
   mushrooms, halved

250 g (8 oz) fontina cheese,
   cut into small cubes

I used to have this as a child as it was cheap and, as my mamma had nine of us to feed, it was easier to make a large amount of polenta and top it with whatever she had.

1 Preheat the oven to 100°C/fan oven 80°C/Gas Mark ½. Cut the tomatoes in half and place on a baking tray, cut-side up. Season with salt, pepper and oregano and drizzle with some of the olive oil. Cook for 1 hour.

2 Cook the polenta according to packet instructions and pour into a 27 x 35 x 2.5 cm (10½ x 14 x 1 inch) buttered baking dish and leave to cool.

3 Preheat the grill. Heat the remaining oil in a pan, add the garlic and mushrooms and cook for 15 minutes. Scatter the mushrooms over the polenta and add the tomatoes. Top with the cheese and grill for 10 minutes until the cheese has melted. Cut into slices to serve.

Zilli know-how

Polenta is made from ground cornmeal which you boil with water to create a 'porridge'. Like most grains, you can get coarse ground or fine polenta. Making polenta the Italian way takes over an hour and you cannot leave it, so the new easy cook, instant polenta is the one I mainly use now. You can refrigerate the polenta until it hardens and then cut and grill it as a base to a dish.

christmas crêpes

FOR THE FILLING
1 butternut squash
100 ml (3½ fl oz) olive oil
3 tablespoons fresh lemon thyme
2 garlic cloves, chopped
1 onion, chopped
1 tablespoon chopped fresh sage leaves
200 g (7 oz) smoked tofu, cut into very small cubes
1 glass white wine
handful of toasted walnuts

FOR THE PANCAKES
75 g (3 oz) rice flour
50 g (2 oz) chestnut flour
2 teaspoons baking powder
½ teaspoon bicarbonate of soda
2 eggs
2 tablespoons olive oil
75 ml (3 fl oz) milk

FOR THE TRUFFLE CREAM SAUCE
3 tablespoons butter
1 shallot, finely chopped
½ garlic clove, minced
250 ml (8 fl oz) white wine
1 tablespoon double cream
1 small black truffle or a little truffle oil

The chestnut flour makes the pancakes sweeter than they would be if you used plain flour. Chestnut flour is gluten free.

1 Peel and cut the squash into 1 cm (½ inch) cubes. Place the squash in a roasting tin, toss in the olive oil, thyme and half the garlic, cover with foil and bake for 15 minutes. Remove the foil and cook for a further 5 minutes – the squash needs to be soft but not overcooked.

2 In a saucepan, cook the onion, sage and remaining garlic in a little oil for 5 minutes until the onion starts to go brown. Add the tofu and cook for 5 minutes. Add the wine and reduce for a further 3 minutes. Remove from the heat and stir in the squash and most of the walnuts. Season to taste and keep warm.

3 In a bowl, mix together the rice flour, chestnut flour, baking powder, pinch of salt and bicarbonate of soda. In another bowl, whisk together the eggs, oil and milk. Add the egg mixture to the flour and whisk until there are no lumps. Set the batter on one side to rest for 10 minutes.

4 Heat a non-stick pan until hot, add a quarter of the pancake mixture and cook until it starts to bubble and go brown around the edges, flip and cook until golden. Make 4 pancakes in total and keep warm.

5 Now make the truffle cream sauce. Heat 1 tablespoon butter in a pan and fry the shallot until transparent, adding the garlic halfway through. Add the wine and reduce by three-quarters, then add the double cream and bring to the boil. Remove from the heat and add the remaining butter, mixing slowly. Grate the truffle into the cream or add the truffle oil.

6 Lay the pancakes on a plate, add the tofu filling and roll up to form a wrap. Pour over the truffle sauce and sprinkle with some toasted walnuts.

vegetable and herb crumble

SERVES 6

FOR THE TOPPING
**250 g (8 oz) sunflower
    margarine**
**425 g (14 oz) gluten-free
    flour**
**2 tablespoons finely
    chopped rosemary**
**2 tablespoons finely
    chopped sage**
**2 tablespoons finely
    chopped thyme**

FOR THE FILLING
3 parsnips, diced
1 celeriac, diced
olive oil
**salt and freshly ground
    black pepper**
1 large carrot, diced
1 onion, diced
1 tablespoon chopped garlic
**2 leeks, cut into 4 cm (1½
    inch) pieces**
100 ml (3½ fl oz) red wine
400 g can chopped tomatoes
**1 litre (1¾ pints) hot
    vegetable stock**
**4 tablespoons chopped
    parsley**

FOR THE CRANBERRY SAUCE
250 ml (8 fl oz) water
225 g (7½ oz) sugar
375 g (12 oz) cranberries

It used to be that you couldn't get gluten-free flour anywhere but now most supermarkets and health stores sell it.

1 To make the topping, rub the margarine into the flour until the mixture resembles breadcrumbs. Stir through the chopped herbs and set crumble on one side.

2 Preheat the oven to 190°C/fan oven 170°C/Gas Mark 5. Put the parsnips and celeriac in a roasting tin, drizzle with a little olive oil and salt, and roast for 10 minutes until tender.

3 Heat a little olive oil in a large pan and cook the carrot, onion, garlic and leeks for 5 minutes. Add the wine and cook for a further 5 minutes. Stir in the tomatoes and cook for another 5 minutes.

4 Add the stock, roasted parsnips and celeriac, and cook for about 10 minutes until the filling is nice and creamy. Season and set aside to cool and for the flavours to combine, then stir in the parsley.

5 Meanwhile, put all the cranberry sauce ingredients into a pan, bring to the boil and cook for 5 minutes.

6 Pour the filling into an ovenproof dish and cover with the crumble topping. Bake in the oven at 180°C/fan oven 160°C/Gas Mark 4 for 15 minutes until golden. Remove and serve the crumble with the cranberry sauce.

baked risotto with tomato and mozzarella

SERVES 4

2 tablespoons extra virgin
  olive oil
50 g (2 oz) butter
4 banana shallots, finely
  chopped
325 g (11 oz) arborio rice
250 ml (8 fl oz) white wine
1.5 litres (2½ pints) hot
  vegetable stock
400 g tomato sauce or can of
  chopped tomatoes
salt and freshly ground
  black pepper
3 tablespoons chopped fresh
  parsley
4 tablespoons freshly grated
  pecorino cheese
200 g (7 oz) mozzarella
  cheese, torn into pieces
4 tablespoons breadcrumbs

Here's a different way with risotto with a crispy top – my kids think it's like a cheesy rice pud and love it.

1 Heat the oil and half the butter in a large deep frying pan. Add the shallots and fry gently for 5 minutes until soft. Add the rice and stir until it is glistening with butter. Pour in the wine and cook until all the wine has been absorbed.

2 In a separate pan, bring the stock to a simmer. Add a ladleful of hot stock to the rice and cook over a moderate heat for 3–5 minutes, stirring, until the liquid is absorbed. Continue adding the stock, a ladleful at a time. Ten minutes before the risotto is cooked, add the tomato sauce or chopped tomatoes and seasoning.

3 When the risotto is ready, remove from the heat and stir in the remaining butter, parsley and pecorino. The finished risotto should be quite fluffy but not soupy. Add the mozzarella.

4 Grease a roasting tin with some butter and sprinkle over 2 tablespoons breadcrumbs, ensuring the tin is covered in crumbs by tipping it from left to right as if you were flouring a cake tin.

5 Preheat the oven to 180°C/fan oven 160°C/Gas Mark 4. Add the risotto to the roasting tin and top with the remaining breadcrumbs, then cook for 20 minutes until golden brown.

vegetable ratatouille
with tofu

SERVES 4
Suitable for vegans

1 onion
1 tablespoon dried porcini
   mushrooms, rehydrated
1 celery stick
½ aubergine
2 bay leaves
1 red pepper, deseeded
1 green pepper, deseeded
1 courgette
4 tablespoons olive oil
2 garlic cloves, crushed
2 tablespoons chopped fresh
   thyme
2 tablespoons chopped fresh
   rosemary
400 g (13 oz) firm tofu, cut
   into 1.5 cm (¾ inch) cubes
400 g (13 oz) passata or
   blended tinned tomatoes
2 tablespoons chopped
   fresh parsley

There is a lot of preparation to this recipe, but once you have it all ready, it's quick to put together for a speedy supper.

1 Cut all the vegetables into 1 cm (½ inch) pieces. Heat the oil in a large pan and cook the onion, garlic, mushrooms, celery, aubergine and bay leaves for 5 minutes. Add the peppers, courgette, thyme and rosemary, and continue cooking the ratatouille for 5 minutes.

2 Add the tofu cubes and passata to the pan, and simmer for 15 minutes. Stir in the parsley and serve with rice or pasta.

cauliflower and saffron cheese pie

SERVES 6

1 tablespoon butter

2 tablespoons olive oil

1 white onion, sliced

1 tablespoon chopped garlic

1 tablespoon chopped fresh
   rosemary

1 tablespoon chopped fresh
   sage

1 tablespoon chopped fresh
   thyme

100 ml (3½ fl oz) white wine

1 kg (2 lb) cauliflower, cut
   into little florets

1 sachet saffron strands,
   soaked in 1 tablespoon
   hot water

150 g (5 oz) blue cheese,
   crumbled

salt and freshly ground
   black pepper

400 g packet of ready-made
   puff pastry

Everyone likes cauliflower cheese and this recipe is just a way to make it into a meal rather than a side dish and means you can enjoy it even more.

1 Melt the butter and oil in a large pan. Add the onion, garlic and herbs, and cook for about 3 minutes. Add the white wine and cauliflower, and cook for 15 minutes until the cauliflower is soft. Add the saffron and continue cooking for a further 2 minutes. Remove the pan from the heat and stir in the blue cheese and seasoning to taste.

2 Preheat the oven to 200°C/fan oven 180°C/Gas Mark 6. Roll out the puff pastry and use some to line a 40 x 20 cm (16 x 8 inch) pie dish or baking tray. Spoon in the cauliflower mixture, and top with the remaining pastry, twisting the edges to make sure the lid is firmly sealed. Brush the top with a little oil and cook in the oven for 15 minutes until golden.

broccoli and parmesan casserole

SERVES 4-6

1.2 kg (2 lb 8 oz) broccoli
  florets, roughly chopped
50 g (2 oz) butter
40 g (1½ oz) plain flour
½ teaspoon mustard powder
350 ml (12 fl oz) skimmed
  milk
250 ml (8 fl oz) vegetable
  stock
salt and freshly ground
  black pepper
100 g (3½ oz) mature
  Cheddar cheese, grated
40 g (1½ oz) grated
  Parmesan cheese
1 red pepper, deseeded
  and diced
75 g (3 oz) breadcrumbs,
  toasted
1 tablespoon chopped fresh
  parsley
olive oil, for drizzling

Broccoli is a real superfood, rich in a wide range of antioxidants, vitamins C and E, folate and iron. A good dish to get the kids eating broccoli.

1 Preheat the oven to 200°C/fan oven 180°C/Gas Mark 6. Cook the broccoli for 2 minutes in boiling water, and drain. Melt the butter in a pan and stir in the flour and mustard. Over a medium heat, slowly whisk in the milk and stock to make a béchamel sauce. Season and add the Cheddar cheese and half the Parmesan, and stir until melted.

2 Remove the sauce from the heat and stir in the red pepper and broccoli. Pour the mixture into a baking dish. Mix together the breadcrumbs, parsley and remaining Parmesan, and sprinkle over the top. Drizzle with a little olive oil and cook for 15 minutes until the top is golden.

vegetable tagine

SERVES 6

Suitable for vegans

1 tablespoon olive oil

2 medium onions, roughly
   chopped

2 celery sticks, roughly
   chopped

6 garlic cloves, crushed

2 cinnamon sticks

1 teaspoon ground cumin

½ teaspoon ground
   coriander

½ teaspoon ground ginger

½ teaspoon ground black
   pepper

½ teaspoon paprika

½ teaspoon ground nutmeg

½ teaspoon ground cloves

2 litres (3½ pints) hot
   vegetable stock

1 kg (2 lb) parsnips, roughly
   chopped

1 kg (2 lb) carrots, roughly
   chopped

1 kg (2 lb) new potatoes,
   halved

100 g (3½ oz) ready-to-eat
   dried apricots

salt and freshly ground
   black pepper

couscous, to serve

This Moroccan recipe is packed with spices, but don't think you can leave any out as the flavour will not be the same.

1 Heat the oil in a large pan and cook the onions, celery and garlic for 5 minutes over a low heat. Add all the spices and cook for a further 2 minutes. Add 2 tablespoons of the stock and cook until the stock has reduced.

2 Add all the remaining vegetables and the stock to the pan, and bring to the boil. Reduce the heat to a simmer and leave the tagine to cook for 1 hour. Add the apricots and seasoning and serve with couscous.

WINTER suppers

macadamia and brazil mushroom roast

SERVES 4

Suitable for vegans

250 g (8 oz) brown bread, torn into pieces
½ bunch parsley
2 garlic cloves, chopped
175 g (6 oz) Brazil nuts
50 g (2oz) macadamia nuts
50 g (2 oz) ground almonds
250 g (8 oz) button mushrooms
1 tablespoon olive oil
2 onions, chopped
½ bunch sage, chopped
½ bunch thyme, chopped
½ bunch rosemary, chopped
2 red peppers, deseeded and chopped
500 ml (18 fl oz) passata
salt and freshly ground black pepper

I love macadamia nuts and this recipe is one of my favourites! If you are not a fan, swap for whichever nuts you prefer.

1 Whizz together the bread, parsley and garlic in a food processor and set on one side.

2 Preheat the oven to 160°C/fan oven 140°C/Gas Mark 3. Spread all the nuts on a baking tray and toast in the oven until golden, stirring often. Whizz the nuts in the food processor and set on one side. Whizz the mushrooms in the food processor and set on one side.

3 Heat the oil in a pan and fry the onions for 2 minutes. Add the herbs and red peppers, and cook for a further 2 minutes.

4 In a large bowl, mix together the bread mixture, nuts, mushrooms and onion and herb mixture. Stir in the passata and season. Increase the oven temperature to 180°C/fan oven 160°C/Gas Mark 4. Spoon the mixture onto a lined baking tray and, using your hands, form it into a loaf shape. Cook for 30 minutes. Serve in slices with the Roast vegetables and Mushroom gravy (see recipes opposite).

roast vegetables

SERVES 4
Suitable for vegans

2 parsnips, cut into strips
**1 bunch baby carrots,
    trimmed**
**1 bunch baby beetroot,
    trimmed**
**2 tablespoons chopped fresh
    rosemary**
2 garlic cloves, chopped
**salt and freshly ground
    black pepper**
100 ml (3½ fl oz) olive oil

*An easy and tempting way to serve
vegetables – roasted with rosemary.*

Preheat the oven to 190°C/fan oven 170°C/Gas Mark 5. Place all the vegetables on a large baking tray and sprinkle over the rosemary, garlic and seasoning. Drizzle with the oil and toss together. Roast in the oven for 20 minutes until tender.

mushroom gravy

Suitable for vegans

50 ml (2 fl oz) olive oil
**1 handful dried porcini
    mushrooms, soaked
    overnight**
1 carrot, chopped
2 celery sticks, chopped
1 red onion, chopped
**1 tablespoon each chopped
    fresh rosemary and thyme**
4 garlic cloves, chopped
250 ml (8 fl oz) red wine
2 litres (3½ pints) water
2 tablespoons cornflour

*Porcini mushrooms add a strong tasty flavour
to this gravy.*

1 Heat the oil in a large pan. Add the drained mushrooms and cook for 3 minutes. Add the carrot, celery, onion, herbs and garlic. Cook for 10 minutes and then add the red wine. Cook until the wine has reduced and then add the water. Cook until reduced by half.

2 Remove from the heat and blend the gravy in a food processor or blender. Sieve the gravy and return to the pan.

3 Mix the cornflour in a cup with a little water and slowly add to the gravy, whisking to ensure there are no lumps. Bring to the boil, season and serve.

WINTER **suppers**

165

poached pears
with chocolate sauce

SERVES 4

FOR THE PEARS
175 ml (6 fl oz) red wine
½ cinnamon stick
1 teaspoon whole cloves
splash of rum
4 pears, peeled

FOR THE SAUCE
1½ tablespoons milk
125 ml (4 fl oz) double cream
25 g (1 oz) caster sugar
2 egg yolks
1 teaspoon plain flour
75 g (3 oz) plain chocolate,
   melted
splash of rum

The secret to success here is to use pears which are only just ripe and not too soft; if they are too ripe they will fall apart and you will end up with a pear mess!

1 Pour the wine into a pan and add the cinnamon, cloves and rum. Add the pears and enough water to cover them. Cover with a lid and poach the pears for 20 minutes until tender. Drain the pears and set aside to cool slightly.

2 Bring the milk and cream to the boil in a pan and remove from the heat. In a bowl, mix together the sugar, egg yolks and flour, whisking until creamy in colour. Add the hot milk mixture to the egg yolks and stir to combine.

3 Stir the chocolate and rum into the sauce and stir well. Pour the chocolate sauce into 4 serving bowls and place a pear in each dish. Serve immediately.

sultana, fig and pecan strudel

SERVES 6

75 g (3 oz) butter
8 fresh figs, chopped
60 g (2½ oz) caster sugar
juice of ½ lemon
150 g (5 oz) pecan nuts,
    chopped
100 g (3½ oz) sultanas
pinch of nutmeg
150 g (5 oz) dark muscovado
    sugar
4 sheets filo pastry
cream or ice cream, to serve

Fresh figs aren't in the shops for long so make the most of their deliciousness in this fruity filo pudding.

1 Preheat the oven to 180°C/fan oven 160°C/Gas Mark 4. Melt the butter and keep warm. Mix the figs, caster sugar and lemon juice together in a bowl and set on one side.

2 In another bowl, mix together the pecans, sultanas, nutmeg and muscovado sugar. Lay a sheet of pastry on top of some cling film and brush with some of the melted butter. Scatter over one-third of the pecan mix. Lay another pastry sheet on top and brush with the butter, scatter with another third of the pecan mix. Top with another pastry sheet and repeat, laying the last pastry sheet on top.

3 Spread the fig mixture along one long side of the filo pastry and brush the other side with the remaining butter. Starting from the side with the fig mixture and using the cling film to help, roll up to form a 'sausage' shape, pressing to ensure the pastry has stuck together.

4 Lift the strudel onto a baking tray, discarding the cling film, and cook for 25 minutes until golden. Cut the strudel into slices and serve with cream or ice cream.

rhubarb and lime tart

SERVES 8

FOR THE PASTRY CASE
100 g (3½ oz) plain flour
50 g (2 oz) self-raising flour
pinch of salt
½ tablespoon caster sugar
125 g (4 oz) unsalted butter
2 tablespoons sour cream
dash of lime juice

FOR THE FILLING
125 g (4 oz) caster sugar
75 ml (3 fl oz) water
zest of 1 lime
1 cinnamon stick
900 g (1 lb 14 oz) rhubarb,
    trimmed and cut into
    5 cm (2 inch) pieces
ice cream or custard, to
    serve

I wasn't sure lime would work with rhubarb but it adds a zinginess to it which tingles the tastebuds.

1 To make the pastry, combine the flours, salt and sugar in a bowl. Rub in the butter until crumbs are formed. Add the sour cream and lime juice and keep mixing to form a dough (it won't be smooth but this is fine). Wrap the dough in cling film and chill for 2 hours.

2 Preheat the oven to 200°C/fan oven 180°C/Gas Mark 6. Grease a 25 cm (10 inch) round tart tin. Roll out the dough to a 5 mm (¼ inch) thickness and line the tart tin; trim the overhanging edges. Prick the base of the pastry case with a fork and cover with baking paper and baking beans. Cook for 15 minutes. Take out of the oven and remove the paper and beans, then cook the pastry case for a further 5 minutes.

3 To make the filling, combine the sugar and water in a saucepan and cook over a low heat until the sugar dissolves. Add the lime zest and cinnamon stick and bring to the boil. Add the rhubarb, bring back to the boil, then reduce to a medium heat. Cover and simmer for about 5 minutes until the rhubarb is just soft. Remove from the heat and leave to stand for 15 minutes.

4 Using a slotted spoon, remove the rhubarb and set on one side. Reduce the cooking liquid by half. Remove from the heat and leave to cool slightly. Remove the cinnamon stick.

5 Place the rhubarb in the cooked tart case and then pour over the syrup. Cook at 180°C/fan oven 160°C/Gas Mark 4 for 15 minutes. Serve with ice cream or custard.

ricotta and chocolate cheesecake

SERVES 12

FOR THE DOUGH
600 g (1 lb 4 oz) plain flour
**100 g (3½ oz) golden caster
    sugar**
5 eggs
240 ml (7½ fl oz) olive oil
1 teapoon baking powder
pinch of salt

FOR THE FILLING
**500 g (1 lb) hard ricotta
    cheese**
200 g (7 oz) goat's cheese
7 eggs
**100 g (3½ oz) white
    chocolate, melted**
2 teapoons baking powder
1 teaspoon ground nutmeg
pinch of salt
1 egg yolk, to glaze

Lovers of white chocolate won't be able to resist this wickedly sensational cheesecake. Perfect for party entertaining.

1 In a large bowl, mix all the dough ingredients together and leave to rest for 20 minutes, covered in a cool place. Cut off ⅓ of the dough and roll into a 25 cm (10 inch) circle. Roll the remaining dough into a 30 cm (12 inch) circle.

2 Place the filling ingredients in a blender or food processor and mix together well.

3 Preheat the oven to 180°C/fan oven 160°C/Gas Mark 4. Use the larger dough circle to line the base and sides of a greased 25 cm (10 inch) springform tin. Spoon in the filling and then cover with the remaining dough, trimming away the excess dough and sealing the edges well. Using a toothpick, prick a few holes in the pastry. Brush with egg yolk and bake the cheesecake for 1 hour. Serve with warm vanilla custard or ice cream.

cappuccino crème brûlée

SERVES 6

500 ml (18 fl oz) double
  cream
1 vanilla pod
15 g (½ oz) ground espresso
  coffee
8 egg yolks
150 g (5 oz) caster sugar
3 tablespoons demerara
  sugar

Combine coffee and pudding with this delicious dessert. Prepare a day ahead and make the topping just before serving.

1 Pour the cream into a pan. Scrape the seeds from the vanilla pod and add the seeds and pod to the cream. Bring to the boil, add the coffee and stir until the coffee dissolves.

2 In a bowl, whisk the egg yolks and caster sugar together until thick and pale in colour. Pour the coffee mixture over the eggs and whisk well. Return the coffee custard to a clean pan over a low heat. Cook the custard until it begins to thicken, stirring continuously, but do not allow it to boil. Remove the pan from the heat and strain the custard into 6 ramekins. Chill in the fridge overnight.

3 When ready to serve, cover the brûlées with demerara sugar and place under a hot grill for 2 minutes until bubbling and melted (or use a blowtorch to caramelise the top). Serve the puddings immediately.

Index

Conversion tables

The tables below are only approximate and are meant to be used as a guide only.

Approximate American/European conversions

	USA	Metric	Imperial
brown sugar	1 cup	175 g	6 oz
butter	1 stick	125 g	4 oz
butter/margarine	1 cup	250 g	8 oz
caster and granulated sugar	2 level tablespoons	25 g	1 oz
caster and granulated sugar	1 cup	250 g	8 oz
currants	1 cup	150 g	5 oz
flour	1 cup	150 g	5 oz
golden syrup	1 cup	375 g	12 oz
ground almonds	1 cup	125 g	4 oz
sultanas/raisins	1 cup	200 g	7 oz

Approximate American/European conversions

American	European
1 teaspoon	1 teaspoon/5 ml
½ fl oz	1 tablespoon/½ fl oz/15 ml
¼ cup	4 tablespoons/2 fl oz/50 ml
½ cup plus 2 tablespoons	¼ pint/5 fl oz/150 ml
1¼ cups	½ pint/10 fl oz/300 ml
1 pint/16 fl oz	1 pint/20 fl oz/600 ml
2½ pints (5 cups)	1.1 litres/2 pints
10 pints	4.5 litres/8 pints

Liquid measures

Imperial	ml	fl oz
1 teaspoon	5	
2 tablespoons	25	1
4 tablespoons	50	2
¼ pint/1 gill	150	5
⅓ pint	200	7
½ pint	300	10
¾ pint	450	15
1 pint	600	20
1¾ pints	1000 (1 litre)	35

Oven temperatures

American	Celsius	Fahrenheit	Gas Mark
Cool	130	250	½
Very slow	140	275	1
Slow	150	300	2
Moderate	170	325	3
Moderate	180	350	4
Moderately hot	190	375	5
Fairly hot	200	400	6
Hot	220	425	7
Very hot	230	450	8
Extremely hot	240	475	9

Other useful measurements

Measurement	Metric	Imperial
1 American cup	225 ml	7½ fl oz
1 egg, size 3	50 ml	2 fl oz
1 egg white	25 ml	1 fl oz
1 rounded tablespoon flour	25 g	1 oz
1 rounded tablespoon cornflour	25 g	1 oz
1 rounded tablespoon caster sugar	25 g	1 oz

AGA conversion – oven temperature to heat

Temperature		2 oven Aga	3 oven Aga	4 oven Aga
°C	Gas mark			
240	9	Roasting Oven	Roasting Oven	Roasting Oven
230	8	Middle Roasting Oven	Middle Roasting Oven	Middle Roasting Oven
220	7	Lower Roasting Oven	Lower Roasting Oven	Lower Roasting Oven
200	6	Grid shelf on floor of Roasting Oven	Grid shelf on floor of Roasting Oven	Grid shelf on floor of Roasting Oven
190	5	Grid shelf on floor of Roasting Oven	Top of Baking Oven	Top of Baking Oven
180	4	Grid shelf on floor of Roasting Oven with cold plain shelf on second runners	Middle of Baking Oven	Middle of Baking Oven
160	3	Grid shelf on floor of Roasting Oven with cold plain shelf on third runners	Grid shelf on floor of Baking Oven	Grid shelf on floor of Baking Oven
150	2	Simmering Oven	Simmering Oven	Simmering Oven
140	1	Simmering Oven	Simmering Oven	Simmering Oven
130	½	Simmering Oven with cold plain shelf	Simmering Oven with cold plain shelf	Warming Oven
110			Warming Oven	
100				Warming Oven

Grill at the top of the Roasting Oven. Cook pizzas, pies and quiches in glass or ceramic dishes on the cast-iron floor of the Roasting Oven for good base browning.